THE WALL STREET JOURNAL.

GUIDE TO
UNDERSTANDING
YOUR TAXES

SCOTT R. SCHMEDEL

KENNETH M. MORRIS

ALAN M. SIEGEL

LIG

PRESS

CREDITS:

Editor
Jason Forsythe

Creative Director
Dean Scharf

Design
Dave Wilder

Production
Robert Chi, Chris Hiebert, David Kelly,
Barnes Tilney, Kwee Wang

Illustration
Krista K. Glasser

Photography
Andy Shen

Film
Quad Right, Inc.

SPECIAL THANKS TO:

Dan Austin, Joan Wolf-Woolley, Doug Sease,
Nancy Travaglione, Lottie Lindberg and
Elizabeth Yeh at *The Wall Street Journal*
Library, Dow Jones & Co.

Art Altman, Karen Halloran, Warren Kissin,
Bruce Schachter, Paulina Schmedel, Warren
Shine, Siegel & Gale, Inc.

American Council on Intergovernmental
Relations; American Institute of Certified
Public Accountants and its Library; Center for
the Study of the States, Nelson A. Rockefeller
Institute of Government; Commerce Clearing
House; Ernst & Young; Internal Revenue
Service and the Public Affairs Offices in
Washington, DC, Newark, NJ, Brookhaven,
NY, Brooklyn, NY and Ogden, UT; Price
Waterhouse; Research Institute of America;
Tax Foundation

PICTURE CREDITS:

The Bettmann Archive, New York (pages 6, 7, 8, 9, 10, 28, 29)
FPG, New York (pages 50, 51,76, 77)
The Image Bank, New York (pages 50, 51, 76)
Internal Revenue Service, Ogden, Utah (pages 31, 32, 33)
Reuters/Bettmann, New York (pages 24, 25)
UPI/Bettmann, New York (pages 11, 27, 28, 29, 36, 39)
The Wall Street Journal (page 36)
The Washington Post (page 36)
The White House (pages 24, 25

Lightbulb Press, Inc., 1185 Avenue of the Americas, New York, New York 10036 Tel. 212-575-0513
FIRESIDE and colophon are registered trademarks of Simon & Schuster Inc.
10 9 8 7 6 5 4 3 2 1
ISBN: 0-671-50235-2
No part of this book may be reproduced in any form or by any electronic or mechanical means, including
photocopying or information storage and retrieval system, without written permission from the publisher,
except by a reviewer who may quote brief passages in a review. This publication is sold with the understanding that the authors and publishers are not engaged in rendering financial, accounting or legal
advice, and they assume no legal responsibility for the completeness or accuracy of the contents of this
book. The text is based on information available at time of publication. Distributed by Fireside, a division
of Simon & Schuster. *The Wall Street Journal* is a registered trademark of Dow Jones & Company, Inc.
and is used in the book pursuant to permission of *The Wall Street Journal*.

LIGHTBULB

PRESS

*C*onsidering that we typically give up more than a third of our income to taxes, it's surprising how little we really know about them. We rarely learn about taxes in school, yet paying taxes is one of our civic responsibilities. And around half of us enlist the help of professional preparers every tax season, either to make sure we're playing all the angles or to have an ally in case the IRS comes calling.

Granted, a tax form can seem pretty daunting. There's unfamiliar language—**exemptions, adjusted gross income, marginal tax rate and tax credits**; a host of instructions with more exceptions than rules, any number of critical decisions to make (to itemize or not to itemize) and seemingly endless calculations.

Since most tax books tell you how to fill out a tax form, but not about taxes, we decided to write this basic primer about the things you should know before you ever pick up your return. We used the plain language style and lively graphics that have made the other Wall Street Journal *guides so popular.*

For example, we talk about how to figure your withholding, the different tax rates we pay, why credits are better deals than deductions, and how to survive an IRS audit, should that dreaded event ever occur. We also provide basic advice for making smart tax-planning decisions year-round.

In preparing the guide, we are deeply indebted to The Wall Street Journal for their ardent support and for the vast information resources they made available to us.

Kenneth M. Morris
Scott R. Schmedel
Alan M. Siegel

THE WALL STREET JOURNAL.

GUIDE TO UNDERSTANDING YOUR TAXES

THE TAX SYSTEM

THE IRS

PAYING AS YOU EARN

CONTENTS

THE ANNUAL RETURN

AUDITS & COLLECTIONS

TAX PLANNING

History of Taxes

"Taxes are what we pay for civilized society."

—Oliver Wendell Holmes Jr., 1904

Taxes figure in many of the oldest written records of civilization. Clay cones found in what is now Iraq indicate that there were heavy taxes there more than 4,000 years ago. Inscriptions made on the Rosetta Stone about 200 B.C. tell of tax immunity for Egyptian temples. Two centuries later came the biblical admonition of Jesus Christ during the Roman era: "Render therefore unto Caesar the things which are Caesar's, and unto God the things that are God's."

blessing for the income and property-tax system enacted by the Florentine Republic in 1427.

ANCIENT METHODS OF TAXATION

The rulers of cities and nations throughout history have demanded that their subjects pay tribute in a number of ways. There were taxes on property, income, status and occupation. Many taxes were

Taxes were collected to build temples in ancient Greece

Clay cones record stiff taxes in Iraq 4,000 years ago

| 2,500 BC | 1400 BC | 600 BC |

References to taxation pop up frequently in early art, literature and legend. Lady Godiva's legendary ride on horseback was part of a successful appeal for tax relief for medieval

Taxes being paid to an Egyptian pharaoh in 1380 B.C.

Coventry. William the Conqueror's *Domesday Book* of 1086 was a census of England designed to ensure accurate taxation. A fresco on a wall in the Brancacci Chapel in Florence, Italy, pictures a divine

paid in kind, with part of the grain, cattle or other wealth that someone raised or produced.

Taxes were used to pay for wars of expansion, to enrich kings and aristocrats,

RELIGION AND TAXES

In the Jewish and Christian traditions, taxation is called **tithing.** Traditionally, tithing means giving the first tenth of all your earnings to your religious leaders. This was also called the **first fruits** offering. It meant that whenever you sold something—sheep, for example—the first tenth of the proceeds went to the state, which in this case was run by religious leaders. Once you paid off the state, the rest was yours to keep.

The first mention of taxes in the Bible comes with Abraham in the Book of Genesis. He gave a tenth of the spoils of his war with the King of Sodom to the high priest of what would later be called Jerusalem. Tithing is also spelled out in greater detail in the Book of Leviticus and summarized in the Book of Hebrews in the New Testament.

to control imports and exports and to crush conquered peoples. Some rulers striving to maintain power used tax cuts to win favor. Others levied to make their states strong militarily, while encouraging trade and individual enterprise.

TAXATION IN GREECE

The first **graduated income tax** was recorded in Greece 2,600 years ago. It imposed the highest rates on citizens with the greatest honors and wealth. Solon, the ruler at the time, also legalized and taxed prostitution and used the proceeds to erect a temple.

About 150 years later, under the statesman Pericles, democratic Athens

rental of goods. An army of scribes registered private property and kept track of taxable products and transactions. The government hired tax collectors and held their possessions as security until they delivered the taxes they were responsible for collecting.

TAXATION IN ROME

Rome's senate and later its emperors were adept at draining the resources of its vast domains. As the empire tottered toward collapse in the 4th and 5th centuries A.D.,

Camels and slaves bring taxes to the court of Darius the Great in Persepolis, 5th century B.C.

Exotic feathers were tax payments in the Aztec culture of 15th-century Mexico

500 BC   125 AD   1050 AD   1450 AD

Lady Godiva staged a tax protest in 11th-century England

Tax collectors working for the Roman Emperor Diocletian accept payment from German farmers

had traffic tolls, harbor dues, import and export tariffs, per-head taxes (called **poll taxes**) on freemen and slaves, a sales tax, license fees and a levy on property with rates rising according to wealth.

The Ptolemy dynasty, the Greek dynasty that ruled Egypt after the death of Alexander the Great, set standards for efficient government and taxation. The rulers protected their own products, such as olive oil, with high tariffs on imports. Peasants paid fees to keep cattle and graze them on common land. Farmers gave as much as half their produce to the state.

There were tolls and poll taxes as well as taxes on salt, catches of fish, legal documents, legacies and the sale and

Rome became infected with an epidemic of tax evasion.

In the 4th century, a special police force was created to examine every man's property. Wives and children were tortured to make them reveal hidden wealth. Eventually, aristocrats refused to accept positions and honors simply to avoid the taxes the positions would bring. Skilled artisans left their trades and ordinary citizens abandoned their homes and found refuge among the so-called barbarians.

In the end, according to Will Durant in *Caesar and Christ,* Rome fell because of decaying morals, failing trade, bureaucratic despotism, consuming wars, declining population and "stifling taxes."

War and Taxes

Taxes were a cause of the American Revolution and the Civil War. They also helped pay for them.

The idea of paying for wars with income taxes came from British Prime Minister William Pitt, who instituted a tax on income in 1799 to pay for Britain's prolonged war with Napoleon. The British income tax remained in force until 1816, a year after Napoleon's defeat at Waterloo. A peacetime economic crisis in 1842 restored the income tax in Britain for good.

TAXATION IN THE NEW WORLD

The colonies in America spent little for public purposes. Colonial government got most of the modest revenue it needed from per-head taxes (called **poll taxes**), property taxes and taxes on products.

In 1643, the colonists of New Plymouth, Massachusetts, adopted a forerunner of the income tax called a **faculty tax**. It was applied to people according to their "faculties," or their property and ability to earn income from commerce or a skilled trade. During the American Revolution, from 1775 to 1783, most of the 13 states levied faculty taxes.

The distant British Parliament's efforts to dominate the colonies through **import taxes** on molasses, sugar and tea intensified the misunderstandings between the New World and the Old and led directly to the Revolution. "Taxation without representation is tyranny" became the watchwords of independent thinkers in the 1760s.

When the two-million-plus American colonists protested against taxation without representation, the British responded with more colonial taxes and sent more troops to the colonies to crack down on resisters. Until then, the colonies had been rivals only of each other.

THE BOSTON TEA PARTY—1773
The colonies' common complaints against oppressive taxes and general British repression united them, spawning the Boston Tea Party and eventually the Declaration of Independence in 1776.

THE FIRST U.S. TAXES

There was no national U.S. tax system until several years after the Revolution. To pay for freedom from Britain, the Continental Congress printed paper money and borrowed money from France—Britain's age-old enemy. When the war for liberty was won, the

THE WHISKEY REBELLION—1794

The Whiskey Rebellion grew out of an excise tax of 30 cents a gallon—at a time when a gallon of whiskey usually sold for less than 50 cents. Farmers in Pennsylvania and elsewhere who grew grain for distilling rebelled, and President Washington used militiamen to suppress them.

> *"... In this world, nothing can be said to be certain, except death and taxes."*
> —Benjamin Franklin, 1789

of 1812 against the British. Still, until Abraham Lincoln's inauguration in 1861, taxes on American property and goods played only a small role in government revenues. Even in 1862, the second year of the Civil War, taxes on imported goods accounted for $49 million of the federal government's total receipts of $52 million.

Taxes on imported goods—also called **customs duties** or **tariffs**—were a bone of contention between the North and the South. Northern manufacturers wanted high tariffs to protect their products against lower-priced imports. Southern planters wanted low tariffs to keep their imported goods cheap.

To help pay for the Civil War, Lincoln approved a three percent tax on annual incomes between $600 and $10,000 and a five percent tax on higher incomes. The rates soon increased to 10 percent on income over $5,000.

Less than 1 percent of the population paid income tax during the Civil War, and income-tax revenues made only a small contribution to the war effort. The Civil War income tax was repealed in 1872.

bankrupt national government defaulted on its debts.

The Constitution of 1789 gave taxation powers to the new federal government. The states agreed to a strong central government with ample power to collect taxes "to pay the debts and provide for the common defense and general welfare of the United States."

Under George Washington and John Adams, Congress enacted a broad system of taxes on carriages, liquor, salt, sugar, snuff, legal documents, bonds and auction sales. A tax on homes, land and slaves was added in 1798.

The third president, Thomas Jefferson, championed the common man and opposed the domestic taxes of his predecessors. He saw to it that many of their taxes were repealed.

In the 19th century, war brought new tax burdens to the American people. Various taxes were revived during the war

ABE LINCOLN'S INCOME TAX—1862
On July 1, 1862, Lincoln signed the most sweeping U.S. revenue act to date. Among its many provisions were an inheritance tax and the first U.S. income tax.

OLD ABE'S UNCOMFORTABLE POSITION

9

The Constitutional Debate

The pros and cons of an income tax continued to divide the country after the Civil War.

In the 1890s, the country became embroiled in a fierce constitutional debate over the government's right to levy income taxes. Farm, labor and small-business groups led by Democrats and Populists in Congress won an enactment of a new 2 percent income tax in 1894. The tax

The new Republican president, William Howard Taft, opposed income taxes. But, fearing defeat in Congress on the issue, Taft and conservative Republican leaders agreed in 1909 to the proposal of a constitutional amendment to permit a personal income tax. The conservatives hoped that

For: "I am in favor of an income tax. When I find a man who is not willing to bear his share of the burdens of the government which protects him, I find a man who is unworthy to enjoy the blessings of a government like ours."
—William Jennings Bryan, Democratic presidential nominee, 1896

THE 16TH AMENDMENT TO THE CONSTITUTION OF THE UNITED STATES

IN CONGRESS, ON THE 3RD DAY OF OCTOBER NINETEEN HUNDRED AND THIRTEEN

applied to corporate net income and to personal income over $4,000, including gifts and inheritances. Like the Civil War income tax, this tax affected only a small percentage of the population, mostly well-to-do Easterners.

Opponents of the new tax, led by Republican business interests, filed lawsuits challenging its constitutionality. In 1895, the Supreme Court rejected the income tax as unconstitutional.

Political moods shifted at the turn of the century. Progressive Republican senators broke with their party's leaders on the income-tax issue. In 1908, his last year in office, Republican President Theodore Roosevelt called for an income tax and an inheritance tax.

the amendment would never be ratified by the 36 states it needed. But the manuever failed.

The 36th vote for ratification was cast less than four years later, in February 1913. Adoption of the 16th Amendment made income tax as much a part of the Constitution as if the Founding Fathers had written it.

On October 3, 1913, Woodrow Wilson, a Democrat who had been elected president in 1912 on a platform supporting an income tax, signed a bill that enacted the modern income tax. The new law was written in 21 sections covering just 16 pages.

THE 1913 TAX

Wilson's new income tax was conceived more as an instrument of social fairness than as a revenue producer. It took effect starting March 1, 1913, and produced just $35 million in personal and corporate tax revenue for the remaining 10 months of the year. Only 357,598 personal returns were filed for 1913.

The basic rate was 1 percent on taxable personal income above $3,000 for a single person and $4,000 for a married person. There was a "super tax," or additional tax, on income above $20,000. The super tax rates rose to 6 percent on income above $500,000, making the highest rate 7 percent.

With the onset of World War I, income taxes soon became the mainstay of the federal revenue system and a major tool for carrying out government policy. After the U.S.'s entry into the war, 2.7 million Americans paid income taxes totaling $180.1 million for 1917.

Against: "What is the difference between a taxidermist and a tax collector? The taxidermist takes only your skin."
—Mark Twain, 1902

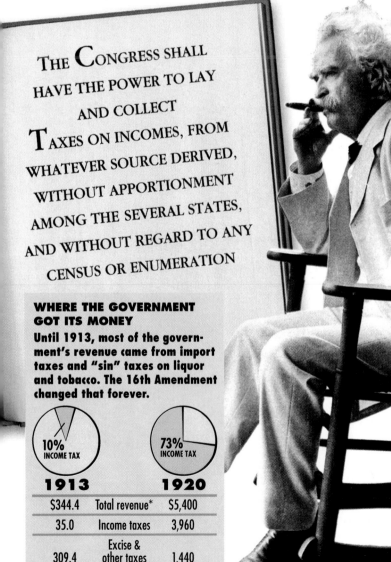

THE CONGRESS SHALL HAVE THE POWER TO LAY AND COLLECT TAXES ON INCOMES, FROM WHATEVER SOURCE DERIVED, WITHOUT APPORTIONMENT AMONG THE SEVERAL STATES, AND WITHOUT REGARD TO ANY CENSUS OR ENUMERATION

WHERE THE GOVERNMENT GOT ITS MONEY

Until 1913, most of the government's revenue came from import taxes and "sin" taxes on liquor and tobacco. The 16th Amendment changed that forever.

10% INCOME TAX
1913

73% INCOME TAX
1920

	1913		1920
$344.4	Total revenue*		$5,400
35.0	Income taxes		3,960
309.4	Excise & other taxes		1,440

(Figures in millions of dollars)
* Excluding import duties

Why Taxes Go Up and Down

While it is certain that taxes will never go away, every now and then they actually do go down.

After the income tax became a permanent fixture in American life, wars proved to be the chief catalyst for income-tax increases. Taxes were raised to pay for the two world wars, the Korean War and the Vietnam War. Taxes were also raised in times of economic stress, as they were in the Great Depression of the 1930s to pay for increased government spending.

Taxes were lowered during peacetime prosperity. They were cut four times during the 1920s and again in 1948, 1962 and 1964. In the 1970s, they were lowered five times.

TAXES SiNCE 1945

After 1945, the federal government sought revenues to help other countries recover from World War II. As a world leader, the U.S. also financed foreign resistance to aggression by the Soviet Union and China.

At home, the government used the income-tax as a lever to promote prosperity, solve economic problems and achieve the American promise of social welfare and equality. As a result, the income-tax laws grew more and more complicated.

But the government also saw the need to make taxes fairer, simplify the rules and block tax avoidance by those clever enough to spot unintended loopholes. These forces were at work in the tax acts passed in the 1950s, 1960s and 1970s.

ECONOMIC THEORIES

Today, tax increases and decreases are the result of political compromises in Washington. These tax debates often pit the theories of the nation's leading economists against each other.

The tax cut of 1981 is a good example of how economic theory can change national tax policy. The tax cut, led by Republican President Ronald Reagan, was guided by a group of economists known as the **supply-siders.** They argued that cutting tax rates across the board would stimulate the economy. The theory was that thriving businesses, invigorated by the tax cut, would eventually contribute more tax revenue than they had before.

TAX BREAKS

Besides tax rates themselves, the chief reason taxes go up or down for most individual taxpayers is the enactment or the repeal of tax deductions, tax shelters and tax credits. Many of these

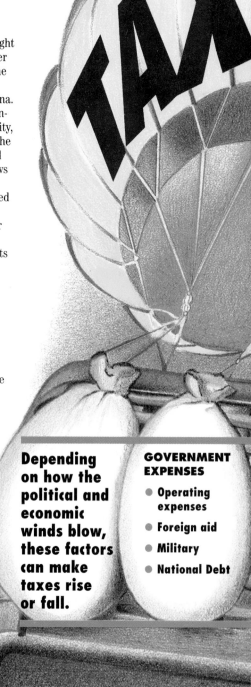

Depending on how the political and economic winds blow, these factors can make taxes rise or fall.

GOVERNMENT EXPENSES

- Operating expenses
- Foreign aid
- Military
- National Debt

tax breaks have worthwhile economic and social purposes. Some goals are to stimulate investment in new businesses, step up research, encourage long-term saving, help charities, ease the burden of medical expenses and promote individual home ownership.

On the negative side, tax breaks tend to distort financial decisions. Consider two families earning the same income and occupying homes of equal value. By owning its home, one family deducts mortgage interest and pays less income tax than the other family, which rents its home. Ultimately, tax breaks divert the course of the economy. People and companies invest and spend money to avoid taxes—not always with the best results.

The effects of tax breaks are often hard to understand. Many ordinary Americans believe the tax system works against them—and for the rich. Consequently, since 1986, curbing tax breaks has become one of the chief objectives of tax legislation. The efforts have been only moderately successful.

THE TAX BURDEN

While tax payments per person have risen steadily in dollars since the 1960s, the tax burden on Americans has stayed about the same. Economists measure tax burden by computing the total taxes paid as a percentage of gross domestic product (GDP). Federal taxes of all kinds took 18.6 percent of the GDP in 1993, not far off the 18.1 percent figure of 1968.

For federal, state and local taxes combined, the story is the same. Taxes at all levels of government claimed 27.8 percent of the GDP in 1991. That figure was in the middle of the range over the previous 25 years.

While the tax burden on Americans has remained fairly constant, sources of revenue frequently seesaw. As one kind of tax is reduced, another is likely to increase. When income-tax rates went down in the 1980s, Social Security and Medicare taxes went up. When the federal government gave less aid to state and local governments, state and local taxes went up.

ECONOMIC CONTROL

- Stimulation of business
- Foreign trade
- Current economic theories

SOCIAL CAUSES

- Welfare
- Healthcare
- Unemployment
- Social Security
- Crime

CONSOLATION PRIZE

Believe it or not, Americans pay less in taxes than citizens of most other developed countries.

Country	Total Taxes as a percent of Gross Domestic Product, 1990
Sweden	56.9 %
France	43.7
Italy	39.1
Germany	37.7
Canada	37.1
Britain	36.7
Switzerland	31.7
Japan	31.3
U.S.	29.9

Source: The Tax Foundation

Tinkering with Taxes

Taxes in the 1980s and 1990s have been altered almost annually by reforms and revenue demands.

Revenue, rates and general tax policy became a prime focus of public and political attention in the 1980s and 1990s. The 14 years from 1981 through 1993 brought eleven major tax acts—including six since 1986.

THE GREAT TAX CUTS OF 1981

The 1981 tax act was designed to deliver the largest tax cuts ever to businesses and individuals. The cuts were supposed to total more than $748 billion over six years.

For individuals, the act lowered the tax rate for the top income bracket to 50 percent from 70 percent and lowered the maximum tax rate on capital gains to 20 percent from 28 percent. The act also cut estate taxes and added incentives for contributions to pension plans and individual retirement accounts.

The 1982 and 1984 tax acts reversed, rewrote or temporarily suspended many major provisions of the 1981 tax act. The two acts also cracked down on tax shelters and provided tougher measures to enforce compliance.

A SURPRISING COALITION: THE 1986 REFORM

A surprising coalition of conservatives and liberals in both political parties came together in 1986 with the common goals of lower tax rates and tax-code simplification. They forged a sweeping bill that made many fundamental changes in the tax code.

Few laws have affected so many Americans as deeply as the Tax Reform Act of 1986. It took four million people off the income-tax rolls and demolished most tax shelters, making it harder for the wealthy to escape taxes. The act also brought the largest tax increase ever for corporations. Key business deductions and credits were restricted or repealed.

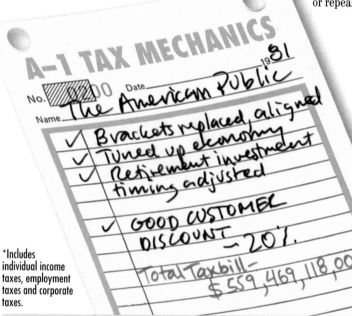

*Includes individual income taxes, employment taxes and corporate taxes.

A-1 TAX MECHANICS 1981

No. _____ Date _____

Name _The American Public_

✓ Brackets replaced, aligned
✓ Tuned up economy
✓ Retirement investment timing adjusted

✓ GOOD CUSTOMER DISCOUNT −20%

Total Tax bill − $559,469,118,000*

RETROACTIVE TAXES

A sore point raised by the 1993 tax act was its retroactivity. The new law was enacted in August, but it raised income-tax rates back to the previous January 1. Many felt that retroactive changes in the tax code were unfair and perhaps even unconstitutional.

Tax historians point out that when the first modern income tax became law in October 1913, it was retroactive to the previous March 1. Furthermore, the U.S. Supreme Court recently upheld the concept of retroactivity.

A-1 TAX MECHANICS
"Tax tune-ups every session of Congress"

A BLOW TO LOBBYISTS

The costs of lobbying Congress and government agencies became a deductible business expense in 1962. Former congressmen and government bureaucrats who could exert influence for special-interest groups soon ranked among the highest-paid people in the country. Meanwhile, businesses represented by lobbyists enjoyed hefty tax write-offs.

The 1993 tax act repealed the deduction for most lobbying activities at the federal, state and local levels.

Main provisions of the 1986 Tax Reform Act:

- The 1986 Tax Reform Act trimmed the number of tax-rate brackets to two: 15 percent and 28 percent. A 5 percent surcharge raised the top effective rate to 33 percent. Previously, there had been 15 brackets ranging from 11 percent to 50 percent.

- It increased personal exemptions and the standard deduction.

- Long-term capital gains on investments were taxed at the same rates as other income. The lower rate was abolished.

- Deductions for sales taxes and for interest on consumer debt—such as credit cards—ended.

- The Act laid more restrictions on deductions for medical expenses, payments to individual retirement accounts, miscellaneous items and interest costs of money borrowed for investment.

- The deduction for interest on a home mortgage was limited to two homes.

- The alternative minimum tax (AMT) paid by people who escaped the regular tax went up by one percentage point to 21 percent.

INTO THE '90s: TAXING THE RICH

The 1990 tax act phased out the benefits of personal exemptions and some itemized deductions claimed by many well-heeled taxpayers.

It also raised the alternative minimum tax (AMT) to 24 percent from 21 percent and imposed luxury taxes on expensive automobiles, boats, planes, jewelry and furs. But it revived the tax break for long-term capital gains and set a maximum rate of 28 percent.

In 1993, a fourth rate bracket of 36 percent was added. A 10 percent surtax at the highest income level created an effective top rate of 39.6 percent. Here are other highlights of the 1993 tax act:

- The alternative minimum tax (AMT) was raised to two tiers—24 percent and 28 percent.

- Some business-expense deductions were limited further.

- The tax on Social Security benefits was raised for upper-income people.

- Pension contributions for upper-income people were restricted.

- Most of the new luxury taxes were repealed—but not the one on expensive autos.

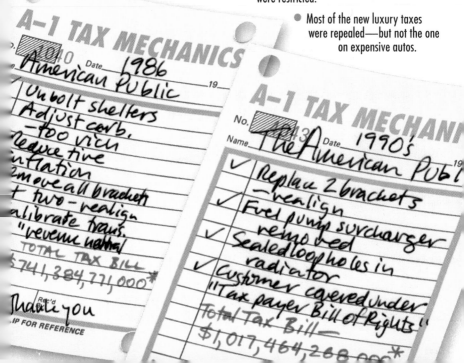

A-1 TAX MECHANICS
No. 1040 Date 1986 19___
American Public
Unbolt shelters
Adjust carb.
—too rich
reductive
inflation
Remove all brackets
+ two—realign
calibrate trans.
"revenue neutral"
TOTAL TAX BILL
$741,384,771,000*
Rec'd
Thank you
TIP FOR REFERENCE

A-1 TAX MECHANICS
No. 1043 Date 1990's 19___
Name The American Public
✓ Replace 2 brackets
  —realign
✓ Fuel pump surcharger
  removed
✓ Sealed loopholes in
  radiator
✓ Customer covered under
  "Taxpayer Bill of Rights"
Total Tax Bill—
$1,017,464,268,000*

Tax Brackets and Marginal Rates

The U.S. income tax is a progressive (or graduated) tax designed so that people pay an increasing percentage rate as their income rises.

The range of income subject to a particular tax rate is known as an **income** or **tax bracket.** For tax year 1994, there are five brackets: 15 percent, 28 percent, 31 percent, 36 percent and 39.6 percent.

The highest rate you pay, on your last dollar of income, is known as your **marginal tax rate.** If you earn enough to be taxed above the lowest tax rate, the **effective** or **average tax rate** you pay on all your taxable income is lower than your marginal tax rate. That's because the amount of income you have in each bracket is taxed at that bracket's rate.

INFLATION AND "BRACKET CREEP"

In times of high inflation, taxpayer income rises, but buying power doesn't. In the past, inflation also meant that rising income nudged taxpayers into higher tax brackets. They paid more tax even though the real value of their earnings stayed the same or went down.

This event became known as "bracket creep." It was, in effect, a hidden tax

Marginal vs. Effective

The amount you end up paying the IRS is calculated by adding the taxes on the share of your income that falls in each tax bracket.

Your effective tax rate may be lower than your marginal rate

For example, the first $38,000 of you and your spouse's combined taxable income of $130,000 in 1994 is taxed at 15 percent. The next chunk of income is taxed at 28 percent, and so on. The result is a percentage of your total taxable income. That number—the overall percentage you pay—is your effective tax rate.

HOW IT WORKS (assume $130,000 of taxable income)

15%	of 0 to $38,000 =	$5,700
28%	of $38,001 to 91,850 =	$15,078
31%	of $91,851 to 130,000 =	$11,826
Tax:		**$32,604**
Marginal tax rate:		**31%**
Effective tax rate:		**25%**

THE 1994 TAX BRACKETS FOR MARRIED TAXPAYERS FILING JOINTLY

Taxable income above $250,000 is taxed at **39.6%**

Taxable income from $140,001 to $250,000 is taxed at **36%**

Taxable income from $91,851 to $140,000 is taxed at **31%**

Taxable income from $38,001 to $91,850 is taxed at **28%**

Taxable income from 0 to $38,000 is taxed at **15%**

WHO HAS PAID AT THE TOP RATES

The following table shows major changes in the top marginal tax rate for individuals since the income tax was adopted in 1913. The tax rates paid by the wealthiest taxpayers have fluctuated widely. Tax rates typically rise during wartime and subside during peacetime. In some years, the rate reflects a surtax or other factors that raise the true marginal rate above the rate stated in the law.

Starting in 1952, the income bracket in the chart is for a married couple filing jointly. Before that, the rates are for individual taxpayers.

Year	On taxable income over:	Rate (%)
1913	$ 500,000	7%
1918	$ 1,000,000	77
1929	$ 100,000	24
1936	$ 5 million	79
1944	$ 200,000	94
1952	$ 400,000	92
1965	$ 200,000	70
1982	$ 106,000	50
1988	$ 71,900	33
1991	$ 82,150	31–34
1993	$ 250,000	39.6

increase Congress didn't have to legislate. Many felt it was unfair. To remedy this, tax brackets, along with the personal exemption, the standard deduction and some other tax factors, have been indexed for inflation since 1985. That means the brackets and other factors are raised automatically every year in proportion to the increase in the cost-of-living index.

Indexing stops bracket creep and even provides a tax cut for people whose income stays the same from year to year.

SOCIAL INSURANCE TAXES

Social Security taxes are called **FICA taxes,** short for the Federal Insurance Contributions Act. For 1994, an employee pays a tax of 6.2 percent on salary up to a ceiling of $60,600. The employer pays an equal amount. (There is no Social Security tax on pay above that ceiling.) Self-employed people are taxed at 12.4 percent, up to the same pay ceiling.

The Medicare tax is 1.45 percent for an employee and 1.45 percent for an employer on all wages and salaries. If you're self-employed, you pay both halves, or 2.9 percent. There is no ceiling for the Medicare tax.

The share of federal revenue derived from these taxes has more than doubled since 1962. That share was 35 percent in 1993, or nearly $412 billion.

THE NO-TAX THRESHOLD

The personal exemption and standard deductions for 1994 were designed so that a married couple with two children and an income of $16,150 would pay no federal income tax.

FEDERAL REVENUES IN 1993

Corporate and personal income taxes along with Social Security taxes produce over 95 percent of federal revenue.

Personal Income Taxes 50%

$586 BILLION

Social Security Taxes 35%

$412 BILLION

Corporate Income Taxes 11%

$132 BILLION

Types of Taxes

Not all taxes are equal: Some take more from the rich; others are tougher on lower incomes.

Flat taxes are the simplest of all taxes because they fall on everyone at the same rate. Besides simplicity, the advantages of flat taxes are that they offer the lowest rates possible and eliminate tax breaks.

While some states have used flat taxes on income, repeated proposals at the federal level have yet to win broad support. This is because flat taxes are **regressive taxes** which shift much of the tax burden away from those with the highest incomes to those with middle and low incomes. A **sales taxes**, for example, is a regressive tax because it is levied on everyone at the

same rate. Sales taxes take a bigger slice of income from poor people, who spend most of it on life's necessities.

The federal income tax is a **progressive tax** because it takes more from those who are able to pay more. The progressive income tax has long been in favor because it is based on the ability to pay.

A **surtax** is a tax placed on top of another tax. It is a way to collect additional taxes on incomes that exceed a threshold without changing the basic tax rate. The 1993 tax act, for example, placed a 10 percent surtax on the highest tax rate.

HOW PROGRESSIVE TAXES WORK

With $200,000 in taxable income

	$ 200,000	Annual taxable income
x	.308	Effective tax rate of 30.8% (marginal tax rate of 36%)
= $	61,600	TAXES DUE

With $20,000 in taxable income

	$ 20,000	Annual taxable income
x	.15	Effective tax rate of 15% (marginal tax rate of 15%)
=	$3,000	TAXES DUE

HOW REGRESSIVE TAXES WORK

With $200,000 in income

$	1,000	5% tax on a $20,000 car
÷	200,000	Your income
=	0.5%	OF YOUR INCOME

With $20,000 in income

$	1,000	5% tax on a $20,000 car
÷	20,000	Your income
=	5%	OF YOUR INCOME

Income Tax

There are many types of taxes beside the progressive personal income tax we are all familiar with.

CORPORATE INCOME TAX

The corporate income tax is imposed on net **corporate income**—total income minus deductions for business expenses. The top corporate income-tax rate generally is lower than the top individual rate. From 1988 to 1992, however, it was one percentage point higher.

Corporations pay income taxes on their profits. Then individual shareholders pay personal income taxes on dividends that corporations pay.

CAPITAL-GAINS TAX

The 1921 tax act first established a lower rate for gains from the sale of assets than for ordinary income. The lower rate for capital gains reflects the strong belief that tax law should encourage investment—particularly in risky ventures—and shouldn't overtax gains caused simply by inflation.

Luxury Taxes

Luxury taxes are excise taxes levied on specific high-ticket purchases. They are aimed squarely at high-income taxpayers, and are therefore a good example of a

tax that targets a specific income group. The 1990 tax act, for example, imposed a 10 percent luxury tax on the purchase of expensive cars, boats, planes, jewelry and furs.

VALUE-ADDED TAX—ON THE HORIZON?

The **VAT**—short for **Value-Added Tax**—is a national sales tax used throughout Europe and in many other countries. It's often proposed as a simple way to supplement or even to replace the U.S. income tax.

The VAT is imposed on sales at each stage in the production of something of value. The tax starts on the sale of raw materials and follows the item through the normal production cycle. Manufacturers, distributors and retailers pay the VAT on their purchases and collect it on their sales to the next link in the economic chain.

As with a sales tax, the total accumulated tax tab is passed on to consumers. In some countries, consumers pay a VAT that exceeds 20 percent.

Many tax experts in and out of government expect the U.S. to have a VAT some day. But at the moment, the odds are against it. Like a sales tax, the VAT is regressive. Beyond that, imposing a VAT increases prices sharply.

A VAT can be complicated for businesses and tax collectors. It interferes with the ability of states and cities to levy sales taxes. Critics also say it would be much too tempting for Congress to raise lots of spending money with what looked like a small VAT increase.

COUNTRIES WITH VAT

Britain	17.5%
Canada	7.0%
Denmark	25.0%
France	18.6%
Germany	15.0%
Italy	19.0%
Japan	3.0%
Mexico	10.0%
South Africa	14.0%
Spain	15.0%

Excise Taxes

Excise taxes are imposed on the manufacture, sale or consumption of certain items. The best-known excise taxes are on tobacco, alcohol, motor fuels, crude oil, automobile tires, guns, fishing equipment, telephone services and airline tickets.

The revenues from some excise taxes end up in special trust funds that are used to improve highways and airports and to clean up hazardous chemical spills. The Treasury's Bureau of Alcohol, Tobacco and Firearms, not the IRS, collects the excise taxes on the products specified in its name.

Sales Taxes

Since the 1930s, 45 states have added taxes on retail sales to their revenue-collection arsenal. Only five states—Alaska, Delaware, Montana, New Hampshire and Oregon—do not have sales taxes.

Although taxes on retail sales continue to creep upward, the most notable trend is to apply sales taxes to more kinds of services. Many states are also trying to force out-of-state catalogue merchants to collect state sales taxes.

The highest sales tax in the U.S. is collected at New Orleans International Airport. The rate is 10.75 percent.

Property Taxes

Property taxes are taxes on the value of property —primarily real estate. Some states have taxes on autos and personal property other than real estate.

Until the Great Depression, property taxes were the mainstay of state revenues.

With the prevalence of state sales taxes, property taxes generally became the province of local governments. Today some 75 percent of the total revenue of all cities, counties and other local governments across the country comes from property taxes.

Estate and Gift Taxes

The federal **estate tax** is imposed on the property of someone who dies if the total value of the property, or estate, is more than $600,000.

The federal **gift tax** is imposed on someone who makes a personal gift with a value above a certain amount. It doesn't apply to charitable gifts. The rules for both taxes are covered on p. 23.

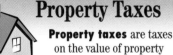

State and Local Taxes

Governments close to home are responsible for providing the major services of daily life.

State and local governments impose a broad variety of taxes on income, sales and property that bring in nearly a third of all U.S. tax revenue. Since 1980, the tax load has moved ever closer to home as the federal government cuts back on its financial aid to states and states have trimmed aid to localities. Local governments' share of all taxes collected from Americans rose to 12.7 percent in 1991—an increase of 15 percent from 1981's share.

STATE INCOME TAXES

State income-tax rates are much lower than federal rates. The structure of state taxes varies widely. Some are flat taxes (see p.18), some are tied to the federal tax, and others are similar to the federal tax, but with variations.

Hawaii, then a U.S. territory, adopted personal and corporate income taxes in 1901, 12 years before the federal income tax. Now 43 states have some kind of income tax. Most recently, Connecticut adopted an income tax in 1991. It was the first to do so since New Jersey in 1976.

Taxpayers in a few states may deduct their federal income taxes on their state returns.

Over half the states don't tax Social Security benefits. Some—including Hawaii, Illinois, and Pennsylvania—exempt all or part of a retiree's pension income from tax. Yet California not only taxes the pension income of its residents, but also demands tax payments on the pension income of former residents who have moved to other states.

Although the income tax generally is considered to be the fairest kind of levy, resistance to it is high in states that don't have one. Seven states don't tax any personal income. They are Alaska, Florida, Nevada, South Dakota, Texas, Washington, and Wyoming. New Hampshire and Tennessee tax only interest and dividend income.

States that don't tax income tend to rely on sales or property taxes. Only two states, Alaska and New Hampshire, have neither income or sales taxes.

WHERE STATES GET THE MONEY

State and Local Tax Revenues for 1991*

SALES TAX **35.3%**

PROPERTY TAX **32.0%**

PERSONAL INCOME TAX **20.8%**

CORPORATE INCOME TAX **4.2%**

OTHER TAXES AND LICENSES **7.7%**

SALES AND OTHER TAXES

Taxes on retail sales and real estate produce the largest portion of state and local revenue. Other state taxes fall on alcoholic beverages, cigarettes, motor fuels, and the extraction of natural resources such as oil, gas, coal, metals and timber.

ESTATE AND INHERITANCE TAXES

Seventeen states still have inheritance taxes, which are paid by heirs on the bequests that they receive. But the trend is toward estate taxes like the federal government's, which apply to a whole estate before its assets are parceled out. All the other states do that.

LOCAL INCOME TAXES

Personal income taxes account for about 5 percent of local tax revenue nationwide. In Pennsylvania, 2,800 municipalities and school districts get revenue from income taxes. Over 1,000 local jurisdictions in 12 other states have income taxes.

These services are paid for by taxes collected by states, counties, municipalities and other local jurisdictions.

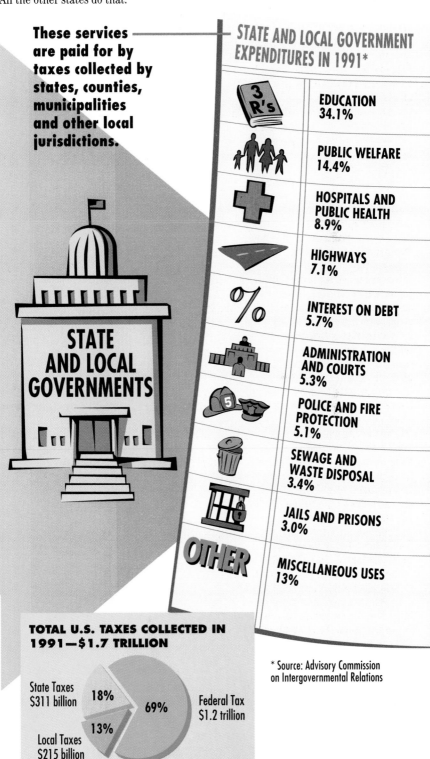

STATE AND LOCAL GOVERNMENTS

STATE AND LOCAL GOVERNMENT EXPENDITURES IN 1991*

3 R's	**EDUCATION** 34.1%
	PUBLIC WELFARE 14.4%
	HOSPITALS AND PUBLIC HEALTH 8.9%
	HIGHWAYS 7.1%
%	**INTEREST ON DEBT** 5.7%
	ADMINISTRATION AND COURTS 5.3%
5	**POLICE AND FIRE PROTECTION** 5.1%
	SEWAGE AND WASTE DISPOSAL 3.4%
	JAILS AND PRISONS 3.0%
OTHER	**MISCELLANEOUS USES** 13%

TOTAL U.S. TAXES COLLECTED IN 1991—$1.7 TRILLION

State Taxes $311 billion — 18%

69% Federal Tax $1.2 trillion

Local Taxes $215 billion — 13%

* Source: Advisory Commission on Intergovernmental Relations

Taxes on the Wealthy

The wealthy must cope with special taxes ordinary taxpayers don't have to pay.

Whether or not you believe that wealthy people pay their fair share of taxes, they pay a much higher percentage of the total income tax collected than average Americans pay.

THE MINIMUM TAX

While wealthy people pay a share of total income taxes that is out of proportion to their numbers, some have been able to manipulate their taxes so well that they pay far less tax than seems fair.

That is because they take advantage of legal tax breaks, called **preferences**, which are significant deductions and credits for expenses that affect only certain kinds of income. Preferences usually involve complex financial arrangements like **incentive stock options (ISOs)**, which give executives the right to buy stock at favorable rates, as well as major deductions for state and local income taxes, tax-shelter losses and the depreciation of business property (activities like drilling and mining are a major category here).

In 1969, Congress tried to limit the financial manipulations open to wealthy taxpayers by enacting a minimum tax. The law now requires that certain people pay an **alternative minimum tax**, or **AMT**. The AMT involves complicated calculations. Taxpayers who benefit from preferences must figure out the tax they would pay under the regular tax rules, and then figure what they would pay under the AMT rules. If their AMT tax bill is

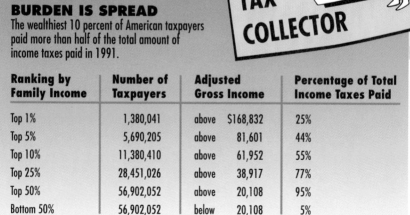

HOW THE TAX BURDEN IS SPREAD

The wealthiest 10 percent of American taxpayers paid more than half of the total amount of income taxes paid in 1991.

Ranking by Family Income	Number of Taxpayers	Adjusted Gross Income		Percentage of Total Income Taxes Paid
Top 1%	1,380,041	above	$168,832	25%
Top 5%	5,690,205	above	81,601	44%
Top 10%	11,380,410	above	61,952	55%
Top 25%	28,451,026	above	38,917	77%
Top 50%	56,902,052	above	20,108	95%
Bottom 50%	56,902,052	below	20,108	5%

GOING PUBLIC

The law forbids the IRS to disclose information about taxpayers to the public. Candidates for public office often choose to release their tax records voluntarily for political reasons.

	Tax year	Adjusted Gross Income	Taxes paid
Gerald Ford	1975	$ 251,991	$ 94,568
Jimmy Carter	1979	195,527	64,944
Ronald Reagan	1987	345,359	86,638
George Bush	1991	1,324,456	204,841
Bill Clinton	1993	293,757	62,670

higher than the regular tax bill, then they have to pay the AMT. Generally speaking, the AMT is harsher than conventional taxes because many of the preferences are disallowed. Therefore, the AMT is something you'll want to avoid.

You calculate the AMT on Form 6251. For more information, see

from generation to generation. This reasoning is still questioned and debated— but the taxes remain.

Estate and gift taxes are known as **transfer taxes.** They are imposed on the privilege of transferring property to someone else, most often a relative. Estate taxes are imposed on the estate; gift taxes are imposed on the giver.

A single rate structure applies to estate and gift taxes. That rate structure applies to estates as well as to gifts made while the donor is still alive. The rates range up to 55 percent on transfers over $3 million.

Gifts and bequests to spouses aren't taxed. Neither is $600,000 of a total estate left to others.

What's Their Secret?

The IRS estimates that 1,219 taxpayers with adjusted gross incomes above $200,000 legally escaped all federal income tax in 1990, the year of its most recent study. And 1,114 of them didn't pay income taxes anywhere in the world.

Unfortunately, there's no secret entrance to the magic kingdom of no taxes. The IRS says these wealthy Americans avoided taxes legally, through a combination of factors, including heavy tax-exempt interest income and substantial deductions for home-mortgage interest, casualty losses and medical expenses.

the instructions for Form 6251 and Publication 909, "Alternative Minimum Tax for Individuals."

The IRS estimates that only 273,000 taxpayers paid the AMT for 1992. But it's likely that several hundred thousand more paid tax experts to calculate whether they owed the AMT or not.

ESTATE AND GIFT TAXES

Historically, estate and gift taxes have been seen as a way to discourage the handing down of concentrated wealth

The law also permits you to give up to $10,000 a year to each one of any number of people without paying tax on the gifts.

Taxes on the personal gifts that people give while they are alive and on the estates they leave after they die provide about 1 percent of federal revenue. In 1993, they came to less than $13 billion.

How Tax Law Is Made

A tax can be fair or it can be simple, but not both.

The conflict between fairness and simplicity arises in the drafting of almost every tax law. Tax experts often cite this rule of thumb: The fairer a tax law is, the more complicated it gets. It's extremely difficult to make a tax fair to everyone and simple at the same time.

The earned-income credit is a good example. It provides tax relief to the working poor. But while it is fair, it is extremely complicated. So complicated, in fact, that many of the poor who use the credit have to pay tax-return preparers to calculate it for them.

THE COHAN RULE: A HISTORIC TAX RULING BY THE COURTS

Entertainer George M. Cohan is remembered for composing "I'm a Yankee Doodle Dandy" and "Give My Regards to Broadway." He has a memorable niche in tax-law annals, too.

When Cohan couldn't produce receipts to support deductions of $55,000, the government refused to let him deduct them. Cohan took his claim to the courts. Luckily for Cohan, a U.S. Court of Appeals believed he had had legitimate expenses, even if he couldn't prove the exact amount.

In 1930, the court ordered the government to "make as close an approximation as it can, bearing heavily, if it chooses, upon the taxpayer whose inexactitude is of his own making."

The decision established the "Cohan rule" which lets taxpayers estimate deductions in certain circumstances. While still a viable rule, taxpayers should not rely upon it. The IRS is increasingly requiring substantiation of claims with paper documentation. And the courts are supporting the IRS.

The president proposes a budget

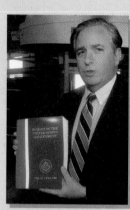

Every year, the president proposes a budget for government spending that usually sets the theme for the tax debate in Congress. The president's Office of Management and Budget plays a central role in developing the budget and advising the president on budgetary matters.

The Treasury Department advises the president on tax matters. An assistant secretary and staff advise the Secretary of the Treasury on tax policy.

Congress writes the tax legislation

The budget proposal is introduced in the House, and the tax provisions are sent to the House Ways and Means Committee for review. Then the president's tax advisers try to work out terms acceptable to Congress and the president.

The Ways and Means Committee and the Senate Finance Committee prepare tax legislation for their respective houses. A bill written in committee is likely to be changed when the House or Senate as a whole considers it.

THE TAX CODE GROWS AND GROWS

When Congress pulled the tax laws together in 1939 to form the first Internal Revenue Code, it created a single volume of 502 pages. By 1993, the code had more than quadrupled in size.

Tax-code pages

Year	Pages
1939	502
1954	927
1986	1,915
1993	2,292

THE STATES' TAX IMMUNITY

The Constitution explicitly bars Congress from taxing exports from any state. The courts have decided that the Constitution also implies that the federal government may not tax state government functions. That's why interest income from state and local bonds is tax-exempt.

The Senate changes or adds to the tax bill

The Senate may debate and even adopt a resolution on taxes before the House does. But the Senate resolution must wait to be attached to a tax bill passed by the House. If the Senate changes or adds to a bill passed by the House, the House may vote on it again.

Usually, if the two houses disagree, they refer the legislation to a third committee drawn from the two tax committees. This "conference committee" works out a compromise to submit to both houses.

The Joint Committee on Taxation drafts the final bill

The Joint Committee on Taxation is a full-time congressional committee composed of 10 senior members of the House Ways and Means and Senate Finance committees. This bipartisan committee has the power to review taxes and their effects. Its large staff of experts advises lawmakers on the technical drafting of tax legislation and estimates the revenue effects of pending legislation.

The tax bill passes both houses and is signed into law by the president

After the House and Senate approve a tax bill, it goes to the president for his signature or veto. Republican President George Bush, for example, vetoed a major tax bill passed by the Democratic-controlled Congress in 1992 because he didn't like several of its provisions.

After the president signs it, the bill becomes law. It is then subject to review by the courts.

The IRS must then interpret and modify the tax forms and its instructions to reflect the new tax law.

THE ROLE OF THE COURTS

The judiciary branch reviews tax law as it does any other law. Taxpayers who dispute an IRS ruling may ask a federal court to interpret part of the Internal Revenue Code in their favor. They may also challenge the constitutionality of a law.

Decisions of the courts that rule on tax legislation or tax regulations become "case law." While the IRS must follow the decisions of the U.S. Supreme Court as precedents for other cases, it may choose not to accept a lower court's ruling as a general precedent.

> **"The power to tax involves the power to destroy."**
> —John Marshall, Chief Justice of the U.S. Supreme Court, 1819

> **"The power to tax is not the power to destroy while this Court sits."**
> —Oliver Wendell Holmes Jr., Supreme Court Justice, 1928

THE GROWTH OF FEDERAL TAX REGULATIONS

Overwhelming as it is, the Internal Revenue Code is just the starting point for many parts of the tax law. The Treasury Department and the IRS are authorized to issue official regulations that spell out the meaning of the code in more detail. These regulations—or "regs" as they are known in the trade—have the force of law unless they are overturned by the courts.

The sheer volume of federal tax regulations has increased over six-fold from 1954 to 1994.

Tax-regulation pages

Year	Pages
1954	1,288
1986	6,248
1994	7,800+

The IRS's Authority

The Internal Revenue Service collects over $1 trillion in taxes every year. It's also the nation's biggest law-enforcement agency.

The IRS, the nation's largest law-enforcement agency, is itself a part of an even bigger government organization: the Treasury Department. The Treasury Department has the job of collecting nearly all of the government's revenue and seeing that people obey tax laws. The IRS is the Treasury's main enforcement arm.

LINES OF AUTHORITY

The Internal Revenue Service collects taxes on behalf of the Treasury Department.

The Treasury Department administers the law and sets tax-collection policy.

Congress creates the tax law.

WHAT THE IRS DOES:

- Creates and distributes the tax forms, instructions and publications designed to help you understand and figure out your taxes.

- Helps you to fill out your own tax return.

- Processes the returns, banks the checks and keeps track of the taxpayer rolls.

- Audits returns for errors and tax evasion.

- Collects unpaid taxes.

- Conducts criminal investigations of tax evaders.

INTERPRETER AND ENFORCER

Congress—not the IRS—has the power to create tax laws. Tax law in the U.S. is called the **Internal Revenue Code.**

Because tax revenue is so vital to the government, Congress has granted broad powers to the Treasury and the IRS to interpret what the tax code means and to force people, if necessary, to pay their taxes. The IRS has broader rights to impose penalties, investigate records and seize property than local police and even the FBI.

IRS regulations and interpretations of the tax law are reviewed by the Treasury. These rules have the force of law unless someone convinces the courts otherwise.

Congress also gives the IRS the authority to grant tax exemptions to educational and charitable organizations.

THE IRS'S IMAGE

The IRS's legal power to interpret the tax code leads to many disputes with taxpayers. Its enforcement powers and its huge work force create openings for error and abuse. As a result, many taxpayers see the IRS as an arrogant, trigger-happy bureaucracy. Some see it as sluggish and behind the times. Many see its dossiers of intimate taxpayer information as threats to privacy and liberty.

In spite of its size, work load, aging technology and largely negative public image, most tax professionals insist that the IRS functions surprisingly well. Many insiders are amazed that the IRS collects such a high percentage of taxes at such a low cost. They are surprised that the IRS's comparatively low-paid employees don't commit many times more errors and misdeeds than they do.

Amazing as it may seem, many IRS-watchers agree that no other tax agency in the world works as effectively for its government and as fairly for its taxpayers.

OTHER TAX COLLECTORS

The Bureau of Alcohol, Tobacco and Firearms (ATF), like the IRS, is a unit of the Treasury. The ATF collected more than $14 billion in excise taxes on alcohol and tobacco products, firearms, ammunition and explosives in 1993. (The IRS collects excise taxes on items like fuel and automobile tires.)

The Treasury's Customs Service collects more than $21.5 billion a year as the monitor of legal and illegal imports and exports.

When the IRS's fiscal year ended on September 30, 1993, it had:

Processed more than 207 million tax returns, including more than 114 million for personal income taxes.

Processed more than one billion other documents besides tax returns.

Collected nearly $1.2 trillion in income, excise, estate, gift, Social Security and other taxes.

Collected nearly $586 billion in personal income taxes.

Paid 81 million personal refunds totaling nearly $84 billion.

Had an operating budget of $7.1 billion.

Had an average of 115,000 employees through the year. Also hired 26,000 temporary workers for the filing season.

Spent 60¢ for every $100 it collected.

History of the IRS

The IRS grew from a four-person operation during the Civil War to one of the government's best-known agencies.

During the Civil War, President Abraham **1862** Lincoln signed sweeping legislation imposing the first income tax in the U.S. The law also created the office of Commissioner of Internal Revenue.

Lincoln appointed George S. Boutwell, a former governor of Massachusetts and later a secretary of the Treasury Department, to be the agency's first commissioner. Working with three clerks in a small room, Boutwell set up field and office forces, wrote regulations and in less than eight months organized the first national tax system. The country was divided into districts, and the president appointed a tax assessor and a collector for each one.

Still, the U.S. financed 80 percent of the Civil War's costs by borrowing, not with income taxes. The rest came from customs and other taxes. By 1872, strong opposition to peacetime income and inheritance taxes succeeded in having them repealed. From then until 1913, the federal government's revenue came from taxes on liquor and tobacco and tariffs on imports.

1872

Although the income tax was repealed in 1872, the newly created tax agency remained. Its job for the next 40 years was to collect taxes on liquor and tobacco.

1953

In 1953, the agency changed its name to **Internal Revenue Service**. The IRS doubled the size of its workforce over the next 40 years.

IRS MISSION STATEMENT

"The purpose of the IRS is to collect the proper amount of tax revenues at the least cost to the public, and in a manner that warrants the highest degree of public confidence in our integrity, efficiency and fairness."

1952

Before 1952, the 64 IRS district collectors around the country were political appointees. But discoveries of widespread corruption led to reforms. "By the end of 1951," an IRS history says, "113 employees and six collectors were forced to resign or were ousted on charges ranging from inefficiency and misconduct to accepting bribes and defrauding the government." In 1952, President Truman and Congress replaced the patronage system with a career service and reorganized the agency and its collection system.

1913

The ratification of the 16th constitutional amendment and the enactment of the modern income tax in 1913 started the Bureau of Internal Revenue on the road to prominence. Few Americans had to pay the income tax at first, but the government's revenue demands during World War I quickly increased their numbers. The number of IRS employees grew more than five-fold, from 4,000 in 1913 to 21,300 in 1922.

1925

Congress cut tax rates five times during the prosperous 1920s. It also directed the tax bureau to help enforce the Volstead prohibition act of 1919. By 1925, more than 3,700 bureau employees were engaged in the war on alcohol bootlegging. Seven tax agents were killed and 39 injured that year.

1943

The revenue demands of World War II led to steep increases in income-tax rates and to a dramatic change in collection methods. Withholding taxes from wages and salaries began in 1943. To handle the bigger workload, bureau employment grew to 50,000 by the end of the war—up from 27,000 in 1941.

1931

In 1931, a bureau undercover agent pieced together much of the evidence used to convict "Scarface" Al Capone, the most notorious gangster of the era, of tax evasion.

RIDE 'EM, COWBOY

Federal tax collectors during the frontier days of the Wild West had to be especially resourceful to perform their job. In 1866, collector N.P. Langford of the Montana Territory improvised his own unique method of dealing with tax dodgers that makes today's methods seem relatively tame. In a letter sent to Washington describing a meeting with two delinquent taxpayers, Langford wrote: "After bearing all I could from them, I...told them not to speak another word in my office or I'd thrash them as they had never been thrashed before. This quieted them and they soon left."

The IRS Workforce

Only 10,000 IRS officials and employees work in Washington. The other 105,000 are scattered throughout the country to process returns and enforce the law.

The IRS's national headquarters in Washington, D.C., sets overall administrative policies. Day-to-day operations come under the seven regional commissioners who are responsible for 63 **districts** and 10 **service centers**.

There is at least one IRS district in each state, with five in California and four in New York. These offices handle most of the direct contacts with taxpayers, including taxpayer assistance, auditing, collections and civil and criminal tax investigations.

FROM THE TOP
The IRS commissioner, who earns $123,100 a year, and the chief IRS counsel, who gets $108,200 as the agency's top lawyer, are the only IRS officials appointed by the president and confirmed by the Senate. Since 1951, commissioners have stayed in office for less than three years, on average.

The agency's other employees, including the deputy commissioner, are civil servants. The deputy commissioner earns a salary of $120,500 a year.

IRS SERVICE CENTERS
The service centers house the computers and the people that process returns. The service centers also keep track of all information reports as

WHO DOES WHAT

Computer Operation

Examination Division

39,000 Employees
The largest block of IRS employees— about 39,000— is assigned to operating and maintaining the computers that process returns and store records.

28,000 Employees
About 28,000 employees are in the examination division, including 15,600 revenue agents who do audits in the field.

A TYPICAL YEAR AT THE OGDEN SERVICE CENTER...

The Ogden Service Center in Ogden, Utah, is one of the 10 IRS service centers across the country. It comprises nine buildings, which house more than 6,000 employees. In 1991, the Ogden Center:

• **Collected $106 billion in taxes.**

• **Mailed 35 million letters—that's one per second.**

• **Received 34,000 returns that were simply unreadable.**

Ogden, UT

Fresno, CA

well as authorize refunds and update taxpayers' accounts.

The centers handle most inquiries about errors and adjustments in taxpayers' accounts. They also send the notices—called CP-2000s—which ask taxpayers to explain why their returns don't show all the income reported to the IRS by employers, banks and other institutions.

The service centers' computers and examiners choose returns for audit. The returns they choose are then forwarded to district auditors.

Other units in the service centers send out a series of notices demanding payment of delinquent taxes before the cases are referred to district revenue officers.

Collection Division	Taxpayer-Service Unit	Tax-Fraud Unit	Chief Counsel

Collection Division

18,000 Employees

The collection division has 18,000 on its staff, including 7,600 revenue officers who track down delinquent taxpayers.

Taxpayer-Service Unit

7,800 Employees

The taxpayer-service unit has 7,800 employees who answer taxpayers' questions and help them with their returns.

Tax-Fraud Unit

5,000 Employees

The tax-fraud unit has 5,000 employees, including 3,100 special agents responsible for criminal investigations.

Chief Counsel

3,000 Employees

The chief counsel's office has about 3,000 employees.

Other

Smaller units deal with taxpayer appeals, company pension plans and tax-exempt organizations.

- There are seven IRS regions, each headed by a regional commissioner and 63 IRS districts.
- There are 10 IRS service centers that process tax returns.

Andover, MA

Holtsville, NY

Philadelphia, PA

Cincinnati, OH

Kansas City, MO

Memphis, TN

Atlanta, GA

Austin, TX

Processing Returns

A combination of people and automated equipment manages the millions of paper returns that tumble out of mail bags into IRS service centers every year.

The IRS is in the midst of an ambitious program to upgrade its technology. At the same time, it is trying to persuade taxpayers that it understands their frustrations and wants to make it easier for them to comply with the law. It says it wants to treat taxpayers like customers.

The chief motivation behind the IRS's program is the widespread perception that the IRS must do as much to encourage voluntary compliance as it does to enforce the law.

IRS GOALS

One of the IRS's main goals is to raise the voluntary compliance rate from 83 percent to above 90 percent by the year 2001. Today, that level seems unapproachable. These are some of the IRS's other goals:

- **Reliance on the telephone for most of its dealings with taxpayers**

- **Instant access to information IRS employees need from IRS files**

- **"One-stop service" for taxpayers**

- **Reliance on electronic filing for most returns**

Returns with payments are dealt with first. The IRS tries to deposit checks within 24 hours of receipt.

1 The envelopes are loaded onto moving belts of 50-foot-long machines. The machines open the envelopes and sort them by reading the bar code on the outside. They put aside returns with payments attached to them by sensing the magnetic imprint on the checks inside. One machine can run through 30,000 envelopes an hour.

IRS PLANS FOR THE FUTURE

To achieve these goals, the IRS says it will reinvent itself by 2001. The measures include a huge project to update computers and automate more functions. The modernization will accompany a major reorganization of the IRS's activities and facilities.

The computer project, called Tax System Modernization, began in the late 1980s and is budgeted to cost $7 billion.

As for reorganization, the IRS plans to consolidate its 70 telephone contact sites into 23 "customer-service centers" designed to provide "one-stop service." To accomplish that, IRS representatives will have immediate computer access to all the information needed to settle most questions and problems over the phone.

Taxpayers will be able to call one of the new centers to get information about

tax laws. On the same call, they will also be able to order forms, straighten out accounts and arrange to pay overdue taxes. IRS aides will call taxpayers to reply to their letters. The aides also will use the phone to get information that is missing from tax returns and to press for unfiled returns and overdue payments.

The IRS also plans to consolidate the operations of the present service centers. Three centers will handle electronically filed returns. The IRS expects that only five centers will be needed for paper returns—thanks to high-tech automation and a steady increase in electronic returns.

Finally, the IRS says that it expects to revise the tax-return forms to make them into what it calls "simple answer-sheet formats that will enhance taxpayer accuracy and ease of processing."

PROCESSING IN 2001

The Austin Center is the pilot site for testing the latest methods of document processing. The first project involves feeding each of the 19 million tax documents that reach the center every year into high-speed scanning machines that store images of the paper returns on optical computer disks. Once scanned in this way, the image can be retrieved on any of the computer screens the IRS uses nationwide to process returns. Once scanned, the paper returns, which currently cost $7 million a year to store in warehouses, can be thrown away.

The Austin center also is working on a pilot program to expand the use of optical character recognition, or OCR. OCR machines can scan the data entered on paper returns and create computer files that can be processed, stored and manipulated electronically. The center already uses OCR to extract data from Form 1040EZ returns.

By the year 2001, high-speed image scanning and OCR are to be extended to four other centers. With on-line information available nationwide, the IRS believes it can create a streamlined one-stop service network.

2 Human sorters take over. Each sorter sits at what is called a Tingle table (named for the inventor, an IRS employee), which is a desk with a double deck of "in" trays around the edge. They separate the returns by type into 20 or more batches. Returns with payments are dealt with first.

3 The next group of workers is responsible for crediting payments to taxpayers' accounts. Another group of workers examines the returns to make sure the necessary entries and signatures are there.

5 After a return is accepted by a service center, the information is recorded on a computer tape, which is sent to the master account file at the national computer center in Martinsburg, West Virginia. The paper returns wind up in storage centers.

4 Keyboard operators sit at terminals to enter basic data from the returns into computer files. This data-entry task is the action most vulnerable to error. The computer helps the IRS verify that a return is acceptable. If it isn't, the IRS will send the taxpayer a letter asking for more information. Taxpayers can greatly reduce the possibility of error by filing their returns electronically.

After the return is accepted, a refund check, if necessary, is generated by the government check-writing agency in Washington, D.C.

Enforcing the Law

The IRS uses its extraordinary enforcement powers to narrow the $150 billion "tax gap."

UNCOLLECTED AND COLLECTED TAXES COMBINED: $1.45 TRILLION

COLLECTED TAXES: $1.3 TRILLION

UNCOLLECTED TAXES: $150 BILLION

The American government depends heavily on what is called **voluntary tax compliance**. That doesn't mean paying taxes is optional, like a good-will offering. It isn't. Voluntary compliance assumes that most Americans are good citizens who are willing to file returns and pay the taxes required by law. The rate of voluntary compliance is estimated at 83 percent, a very high rate compared with most other countries.

The annual **tax gap** represents taxes on income from legal sources that isn't paid because of taxpayer error, confusion or outright evasion. The IRS estimates that the $150 billion gap in 1993 was about two-thirds personal taxes and one-third corporate taxes. The agency doesn't publish estimates of taxes lost on income from illegal sources.

No one is sure how accurate the compliance and tax gap estimates are. Nor does anyone know precisely how much of the money owed to the IRS is collectible—although it is clear that a significant portion will never be collected. Audits and enforcement programs are the IRS's tools for narrowing the gap between what taxpayers owe and what they pay.

According to the IRS commissioner, a 1 percent increase in tax compliance would have added as much as **$10 BILLION** to the government's 1993 revenues.

THE IRS'S POWERS

Federal law places the burden of maintaining tax records, filing an accurate return and paying the correct tax on each taxpayer. The law gives the IRS unusual powers to enforce compliance. Federal courts have upheld these powers.

First, the IRS has a right to see your tax-related records. If you don't provide them, the IRS may issue a summons ordering you or someone else to turn them over. This power must be used only to determine what tax is owed, and can't be used in a criminal investigation.

Second, the IRS may impose a long list of **civil penalties** for such things as failing to file a return, failing to pay tax on time, civil fraud and negligence. Civil fraud isn't as serious a violation—or as hard to prove—as criminal fraud.

The IRS may add a civil penalty to your tax bill without taking you to court. It's up to you to appeal the penalty to an IRS appeals officer or to a court.

Third, the IRS has the right to seize the assets of anyone who doesn't pay the taxes they owe. The IRS must first go through a series of procedural steps, sending notices that give you time to challenge the tax bill in court. But once it has determined that you owe the tax and haven't met the final payment deadline, the IRS may act on its own. It generally doesn't have to get a court order first.

The IRS may file a notice of a **lien** on your property. With a lien, if the property is sold, the IRS claims a share of the proceeds before you do.

The IRS may impose a **levy** on your assets held by other parties. That means the IRS can take part of your regular pay, plus bank accounts and stock held in brokerage accounts

In a process called **distraint**, the IRS may seize a physical asset, such as a car or a home, and sell it. The IRS keeps enough to pay the tax bill and you get the rest, if any. A certain amount of pay and some belongings are safe from levy and distraint. The IRS must obtain a

IRS POWERS IN ACTION

In fiscal year 1993, IRS collection agents filed 959,000 notices of liens on property and nearly 2.6 million notices of levies on property. IRS revenue officers made 10,000 seizures of property.

court order if it wants to force its way onto private premises without your permission.

The IRS has special powers if it believes that you are about to hide property to prevent the collection of tax. In that case, the IRS may skip all administrative and court procedures and seize the property immediately. This is known as a **jeopardy assessment**.

THE DEPARTMENT OF JUSTICE

The federal government's legal arm, the Department of Justice, has a staff of attorneys who specialize in taxes. They represent the United States and the IRS in court in all criminal and many civil tax cases. The Justice Department decides whether to bring criminal charges in tax cases after listening to the IRS's recommendations. IRS lawyers defend the IRS against taxpayers' suits in the U.S. Tax Court. The U.S. Tax Court doesn't hold criminal-case trials.

Crime Fighters

The IRS can use its unique powers to put otherwise elusive criminals behind bars.

The IRS's gun-toting special agents, although a small group, are among the most effective crime investigators in the country.

Adding tax evasion to other charges can increase the pressure on criminals. As in the famous Al Capone case, the government can use the tax laws to go after mobsters and other crooks whose non-tax crimes are hard to prove. The government has long used the IRS in the battle against Capone's successors in organized crime—especially in uncovering **money laundering** associated with the illegal drug trade and other contraband. Money-laundering schemes route illegally acquired cash through legitimate bank accounts and businesses to make the money appear as though it had been earned honestly.

Undercover sleuthing by IRS special agents not only targets suspected thugs. IRS special agents uncovered evidence that forced Vice President Spiro Agnew to plead no contest to charges of evading taxes on alleged bribes. The charges led to his resignation as vice president.

On the negative side, many IRS insiders, including present and former IRS officials, say the government diverts too much of the IRS's money and resources away from its main job. These critics say the IRS should concentrate on encouraging tax compliance and deterring general tax fraud and leave organized crime to the police and the FBI. The critics favor a policy more like the one used as recently as 1980, when only 29 percent of the IRS's crime investigations involved illegal income. Today, that percentage is much higher.

Dave Beck, Former Teamster Presi

Receives $60,000 Fine and Sentence of 5 Years

TACOMA, WASHINGTON, February 27 — Dave Beck, best known as the former president of the International Teamsters Union, was sentenced to a five year prison term along with a fine of $60,000 for not paying $240,000 in Federal income tax.

Dave Beck plans to appeal this decision. He currently has a fifteen year prison sentence imposed by the King County State Court in appeals court also. He was convicted of taking the proceeds, approximately $1,900, from the sale of a Cadillac owned by the union. A hearing has been set for

IRS GUMSHOES

In fiscal year 1993, IRS special agents began 6,146 investigations. About 46 percent of them—or 2,866—involved narcotics, organized crime, the suspected corruption of public officials and other crimes besides tax evasion. IRS investigations led to prison terms for 1,307 tax criminals.

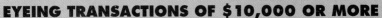

EYEING TRANSACTIONS OF $10,000 OR MORE

Federal law requires banks and businesses to report deposits and payments of more than $10,000 in cash. The reports go to the IRS, which investigates those it considers questionable. IRS agents recently used these reports to uncover a mammoth currency scam. A bank alerted the IRS to a series of suspicious large cash deposits. The investigation led to the arrest in June 1994 of a trusted employee of the U.S. Bureau of Engraving and Printing—the branch of the federal government that prints U.S. currency. He was charged with the largest theft from the bureau in its history—$1.7 million in brand new $100 bills.

freighter. In one four-month period, members were arrested for possessing no less than 33 tons of marijuana.

The church appealed its huge tax bill to the U.S. Tax Court. Church members argued in court that they used marijuana only as a sacrament in their services. According to the judge, the amount recovered—33 tons—made their case ludicrous, and he sided with the IRS.

The result: The judge ordered the church to pay the IRS's claims for taxes and civil penalties, plus $5,000 for making "absurd and frivolous" arguments in court.

WHO POLICES THE IRS

The main responsibility for keeping the IRS on the right track falls on the House Ways and Means Committee and the Senate Finance Committee. Subcommittees regularly hold public hearings on how well the IRS conducts its affairs. On occasion, they hold hearings on charges of IRS abuse.

The committees rely on a congressional investigative agency, the General Accounting Office, or GAO. The GAO monitors IRS operations and issues frequent public reports on the IRS's successes and failures.

The main defense against corruption is the IRS's own internal security office. In fiscal year 1993, this office began 3,180 investigations of possible crimes involving IRS employees and outsiders. The year ended with 188 convictions, including 44 for theft and 31 for bribery. Twelve of the convictions were of private citizens who were caught impersonating IRS agents.

Taxpayers who suspect an IRS employee of improper behavior should call 800-366-4484 to report it. That special number is for the IRS's internal security office. It should also be used if you suspect that someone may be posing as an IRS employee.

WHETHER THE INCOME IS LEGAL OR ILLEGAL—YOU STILL OWE TAXES ON IT.

CONVICTED CRIMINALS STILL PAY THE IRS

Conviction for a tax crime isn't the last word in the pursuit of a tax-law violator. After the criminal case is wrapped up, the IRS goes after the tax itself in a civil proceeding.

That's exactly what happened in the case of the Zion Coptic Church, Inc. of Miami, Florida. The IRS revoked the church's tax exemption after nine members were convicted of possessing marijuana with the intent to distribute it. The IRS said the church acted as a front for a huge drug-smuggling business which owed a whopping tax of $833,747 on its illegal income in one year alone. IRS evidence showed that church members had bought a 153-foot-long sea-going

Withholding

Taxes withheld from your wages keep the government running—and protect you from a big tax bill on April 15.

It's not easy saving money for an entire year to pay your taxes. Without withholding, that's what you'd have to do. For people who like to spend everything they earn, April 15 can be a harrowing day. By giving up a small amount from each paycheck, you are pre-paying your yearly tax bill in installments—and ensuring that April 15 will come and go peacefully.

For the IRS, withholding ensures that it'll get its money—and a steady flow of it—on time.

But unlike other installment plans,

HOW WITHHOLDING WORKS

Withholding gives employers the main responsibility for collecting taxes. They calculate how much of each employee's salary goes to the government, subtract

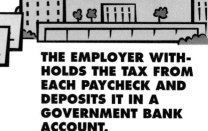

THE EMPLOYER WITH-HOLDS THE TAX FROM EACH PAYCHECK AND DEPOSITS IT IN A GOVERNMENT BANK ACCOUNT.

IF TOO MUCH IS WITHHELD, EMPLOYEE GETS A REFUND

IF TOO LITTLE IS WITHHELD, EMPLOYEE OWES MORE TAX

withholding taxes never stop. You've already started to pay next year's taxes by the time you settle last year's bill on April 15.

A BAD WAY TO SAVE

Many people deliberately have extra tax withheld to build up a big refund. Using withholding as a savings plan, though, is really like giving an interest-free loan to Uncle Sam. The refund is simply money you could have kept for yourself all along. When the government has it, you lose whatever you could have earned by investing it.

Even if you don't think you have the will power to save on your own, tax advisers still say it's better to have to pay a little on April 15. That way, you will enjoy the benefit of an interest-free loan from the government rather than the other way around. But be careful—if you don't withhold enough, you may be subject to penalties and interest.

a portion of each paycheck and deposit the money in government bank accounts. At the end of the year, they issue each employee a W-2 form that reports the total amount withheld and send a copy to the IRS.

The system is designed to help people budget their finances so that they have enough on hand to pay their taxes. At the same time, it simplifies the government's role as tax collector, shifting the bookkeeping, depositing and reporting responsibilities to employers.

HOW MUCH TO WITHHOLD?

It's up to you to provide your employer with the basic information about how much to withhold from your pay. You do that by filling out the IRS Form W-4, "Employee's Withholding Allowance Certificate," given to you by your employer.

On the W-4, you indicate your filing status by choosing either the tax rate for unmarried taxpayers or the lower married rate, and then you indicate any additional money you want withheld to cover non-salary income.

You also list the number of **allowances** you are claiming (see p. 41) Each allowance represents an exemption or some other tax benefit you plan to claim on your tax return. The more allowances you have, the bigger your take-home check will be. You can estimate the right number of allowances by using the W-4 worksheets.

If you don't fill out a W-4, taxes must be withheld at the highest rate—as though you were single and had no allowances.

Ideally, what's withheld will equal what you owe by the end of the year— give or take a few dollars. The IRS imposes a penalty if the amount withheld falls too short.

OVERPAYING AS WE GO
Americans are accustomed to prepaying more money than they later end up owing in taxes. Taxpayers had $410 billion withheld from their paychecks in 1992, the most recent year for which statistics are available. When that number is added to the $112.5 billion Americans pre-paid in estimated taxes, the total is more than all the taxes that individuals owed for the year.

Some 71 percent of personal tax returns filed for that year claimed refunds. Total refunds amounted to $84 billion, making the average refund for each taxpayer $1,033.

WHO SEES YOUR W-4?
Your W-4 usually goes just to your employer. However, if you claim more than 10 withholding allowances, or no withholding at all on wages of more than $200 a week, your employer must send a copy of your W-4 to the IRS. You can head off an IRS inquiry by providing supporting information to your employer. If the IRS disagrees with your claim, it can have your employer withhold tax at a level it sets until your dispute is resolved.

ESCAPING WITHHOLDING
Certain low-income taxpayers can avoid federal withholding taxes for one year. They must first certify that they don't expect to pay any tax at all for the year and show that they didn't have to pay any tax for the previous year. Avoiding withholding is smart for students with low-paying part-time or summer jobs.

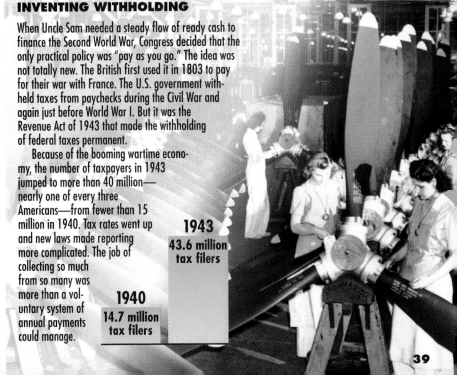

INVENTING WITHHOLDING
When Uncle Sam needed a steady flow of ready cash to finance the Second World War, Congress decided that the only practical policy was "pay as you go." The idea was not totally new. The British first used it in 1803 to pay for their war with France. The U.S. government withheld taxes from paychecks during the Civil War and again just before World War I. But it was the Revenue Act of 1943 that made the withholding of federal taxes permanent.

Because of the booming wartime economy, the number of taxpayers in 1943 jumped to more than 40 million— nearly one of every three Americans—from fewer than 15 million in 1940. Tax rates went up and new laws made reporting more complicated. The job of collecting so much from so many was more than a voluntary system of annual payments could manage.

1943
43.6 million tax filers

1940
14.7 million tax filers

Filling Out the W-4

The W-4 is deceptively brief and mighty complicated.

You must fill out a W-4 when you go to work for a new employer. It's also wise to review your withholding periodically (once a year is a good idea). Hand in a new W-4 when milestones in your life—marriage, the birth or loss of a dependent, big changes in pay, buying a home—may affect your taxes. You must complete a new W-4 within 10 days after a divorce or any other event that may increase your withholding. Also, changes in tax law often require new withholding calculations.

To fill out a W-4 correctly, you'll need basic information about your income and deductible expenses, so it's a good idea to have your latest tax return and the stub of your most recent paycheck on hand.

FACTORS THAT INCREASE WITHHOLDING TAXES

- Having more than one job
- Both spouses working
- Income high enough to limit deductions and exemptions for dependents
- Divorce
- Loss of a dependent who gets other support or who dies

FACTORS THAT DECREASE WITHHOLDING TAXES

- Filing as a single head of household or jointly as a married couple
- Claiming a large number of dependents
- Substantial home-ownership deductions for mortgage interest and real-estate taxes
- High deductions for state and local income taxes
- Substantial credits for child care

The object is to withhold at least 90% of what you think you will owe on April 15—and not much more

----- Cut

Form **W-4**
Department of the Treasury
Internal Revenue Service

1 Type or print your first na
Cynthia

umber a
6 +

e and Z
Tov

f allowa
unt, if

7 I claim exemption from
 • Last year I had a ri
 • This year I expect a
If you meet both con

Under penalties of perjury, I certi

Employee's signature ▶

8 Employer's name and add
AnyCo. USA
123 4th Avenu
New York, NY

INVESTMENT INCOME

A good way to cushion the tax you'll soon face on any income not subject to withholding—such as interest and dividends—is to have more tax withheld from your paycheck. Consider this strategy if you have a lot of interest income or a big capital gain from selling stock.

If you feel too much or too little is being withheld, use a W-4 to refigure your withholding for the rest of the year.

WITHHOLDING ALLOWANCES

Using worksheets that come with the W-4, you estimate the amounts that will probably reduce your taxes—such as exemptions for dependents, deductions for various expenses and tax credits for special costs you incur. Each of these is converted into a **withholding allowance**. Each withholding allowance reduces the amount of tax your employer withholds.

You give the W-4 (but not the worksheets) to your employer. The employer uses this information and IRS tables to determine how much tax to withhold from the amount you earn. (You don't put the amount of your pay on the W-4.)

You enter your filing status on the W-4 by checking off the single-tax-rate box or the lower married-rate box.

You also show the number of allowances and any additional amounts you want withheld.

give the certificate to your employer. Keep the top portion for your records.

loyee's Withholding Allowance Certificate

OMB No. 1545-0010

1994

or Privacy Act and Paperwork Reduction Act Notice, see reverse.

le initial	Last name		2 Your social security number
3.	Gitter		123 : 45 : 6789

ural route)
venue

3 ☐ Single ☒ Married ☐ Married, but withhold at higher Single rate.
Note: If married, but legally separated, or spouse is a nonresident alien, check the Single box.

Y 10036

4 If your last name differs from that on your social security card, check here and call 1-800-772-1213 for more information . . . ▶ ☐

re claiming (from line G above or from the worksheets on page 2 if they apply) . | 5 | 5
vant withheld from each paycheck . . . . | 6 | $ 80—

g for 1994 and I certify that I meet **BOTH** of the following conditions for exemption:
fund of **ALL** Federal income tax withheld because I had **NO** tax liability; **AND**
f **ALL** Federal income tax withheld because I expect to have **NO** tax liability.
ter "EXEMPT" here . . . . ▶ | 7

entitled to the number of withholding allowances claimed on this certificate or entitled to claim exempt status.

ynthin Gitter   Date ▶ Jan. 5 , 19 94

er: Complete 8 and 10 only if sending to the IRS)

	9 Office code (optional)	10 Employer identification number
	101	11213

Cat. No. 10220Q

W-4 Worksheets

The worksheets that come with the W-4 can be a strenuous exercise in tax planning.

Personal Allowances Worksheet

A   Enter "1" for **yourself** if no one else can claim you as a dependent . . . .

B   Enter "1" if:
- You are single and have only one job; or
- You are married, have only one job, and your spouse does not work; or
- Your wages from a second job or your spouse's wages (or the total of both) are $

C   Enter "1" for your **spouse**. But, you may choose to enter -0- if you are married and have eith
more than one job (this may help you avoid having too little tax withheld) . . . . .

D   Enter number of **dependents** (other than your spouse or yourself) whom you will claim on your

E   Enter "1" if you will file as **head of household** on your tax return (see conditions under **Head**

F   Enter "1" if you have at least $1,500 of **child or dependent care expenses** for which you pla

G   Add lines A through F and enter total here. **Note:** This amount may be different from the number of exemptions

For accuracy, do all worksheets that apply.
- If you plan to **itemize or claim adjustments to income** and want to redu and Adjustments Worksheet on page 2.
- If you are **single** and have **more than one job** and your combined earni you are **married** and have a **working spouse or more than one job**, and the $50,000, see the Two-Earner/Two-Job Worksheet on page 2 if you want to
- If **neither** of the above situations applies, **stop here** and enter the number fr

DEDUCTIONS AND ADJUSTMENTS

If you expect to itemize deductions and make adjustments to your income on your return, be sure to fill out this worksheet. It deals with your deductions and adjustments for such expenses as home mortgage interest, state and local income taxes, medical treatment and deposits in IRAs.

Note: Use this worksheet only if you plan t

1   Enter an estimate of your 1994 itemize charitable contributions, state and local of your income, and miscellaneous d deductions if your income is over $111,8

2   Enter:
- $6,350 if married filing jointly
- $5,600 if head of household
- $3,800 if single
- $3,175 if married filing separ

3   **Subtract** line 2 from line 1. If line 2 is g

4   Enter an estimate of your 1994 adjustments t

5   **Add** lines 3 and 4 and enter the total .

6   Enter an estimate of your 1994 nonwage

7   **Subtract** line 6 from line 5. Enter the res

8   **Divide** the amount on line 7 by $2,500 a

9   Enter the number from Personal Allowan

10 **Add** lines 8 and 9 and enter the total here this total on line 1, below. Otherwise, **stop**

Two-Earner/Two-Job Worksheet

Note: Use this worksheet only if the instructions for line G on page 1 direct you here.

1   Enter the number from line G on page 1 (or from line 10 above if you used the Deductions and Adjustme

2   Find the number in **Table 1** below that applies to the **LOWEST** paying job and enter it he

3   If line 1 is **GREATER THAN OR EQUAL TO** line 2, subtract line 2 from line 1. Enter the zero, enter -0-) and on Form W-4, line 5, on page 1. **DO NOT** use the rest of this worksh

Note: If line 1 is **LESS THAN** line 2, enter -0- on Form W-4, line 5, on page 1. Complete lines the additional withholding amount necessary to avoid a year-end tax bill.

4   Enter the number from line 2 of this worksheet . . . .   4 —

5   Enter the number from line 1 of this worksheet . . . .   5 —

6   **Subtract** line 5 from line 4

7   Find the amount in **Table 2** below that applies to the **HIGHEST** paying job and enter

8   **Multiply** line 7 by line 6 and enter the result here. This is the additional annual withhold

9   **Divide** line 8 by the number of pay periods remaining in 1994. (For example, divide b every other week and you complete this form in December 1993.) Enter the result he line 6, page 1. This is the additional amount to be withheld from each paycheck .

WORKSHEETS THAT DON'T COME WITH THE W-4

The main worksheet in Publication 919, "Is My Withholding Correct?" is much more detailed than the worksheets on the W-4. This publication is very useful for upper-income taxpayers, especially for two working spouses or a single person with more than one job. That's because the tax laws limit your itemized deductions and your personal allowances for dependents if your income exceeds certain amounts.

This booklet is also helpful if you receive a lot of income from self-employment or from other sources that are not wages.

You can pick up Publication 919 at your nearest IRS office or you can order one by telephoning 800-829-3676.

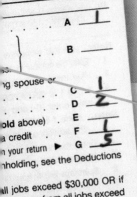

PERSONAL ALLOWANCES

The first W-4 worksheet covers your filing status as a single or married person. It also accounts for your children and any other dependency exemptions.

If your spouse works and you file a joint return, the two of you may not have enough tax withheld. Therefore, you may boost your withholding by not taking an allowance for your spouse.

s and Adjustments Worksheet

eductions or claim adjustments to income on your 1994 tax return.
ns. These include: qualifying home mortgage interest, not sales taxes), medical expenses in excess of 7.5% (For 1994, you may have to reduce your itemized 0 if married filing separately). Get Pub. 919 for details.)

ing widow(er)	1	$ 12,000
	2	$ 6,350
line 1, enter -0-	3	$ 5,650
These include alimony paid and deductible IRA contributions	4	$ 2,000
	5	$ 7,650
such as dividends or interest)	6	$ 1,000
ot less than -0-	7	$ 650
he result here. Drop any fraction	8	0
sheet, line G, on page 1	9	5
in to use the Two-Earner/Two-Job Worksheet, also enter enter this total on Form W-__, on page 1.	10	5

IF YOU HAVE MORE THAN ONE JOB

If you work two or more jobs, the two-earner/two-job worksheet helps you calculate the total additional tax that needs to be withheld. The IRS says that your overall withholding will usually be most accurate if you enter all allowances on the W-4 for the highest-paying job. Then you claim zero allowances on the W-4s for the other jobs. The worksheet on the back of the W-4 helps if:

- **You are single, have more than one job, and earn a total of more than $30,000 a year**

- **You are married, have more than one job or a working spouse and your combined earnings exceed $50,000 a year**

The Long Arms of Withholding

Withholding is the government's not so subtle way of making sure you pay your share of income tax up front.

Withholding has become the most efficient way for the government to collect taxes. Over the years, Congress has stretched withholding's reach beyond wages and salaries to other kinds of income. For the government, withholding has the double advantage of speeding the flow of tax revenue and of frustrating people who otherwise might neglect—or avoid—paying up.

INCOME WITHHOLDING
- Federal income tax
- State unemployment insurance tax
- Local income tax
- Social Security tax
- Medicare tax

JOB-RELATED INCOME
Job-related income is usually included in the gross pay reported on your W-2 (see p. 60). Taxes on the following kinds of income are withheld at the same rates as for wages and salaries:

- Tips, which workers must report to their employers
- Taxable fringe benefits, such as the personal use of a company car
- Sick pay
- Vacation pay
- Severance pay
- Bonuses and commissions (employers may choose to withhold taxes on bonuses and commissions at a flat rate of 28 percent—not the gross pay rate)

STATE AND LOCAL TAXES
State and local governments that tax income also require withholding. You can determine your withholding for state and city purposes by using forms similar to the federal W-4.

PENSIONS AND ANNUITIES
Tax is usually withheld from periodic pension and annuity payments. This withholding applies to income from IRAs, too.

Of course, part of your retirement income may not be taxable at all because it's simply the payout of previously taxed money that you invested in the retirement plan. To figure how much tax should be withheld from retirement income, fill out Form W-4P, "Withholding Certificate for Pension or Annuity Payments," or a similar form supplied by the organization making the retirement payments.

If you receive all of your pension or annuity payments within one year, the payer usually withholds tax at a 10 percent rate. That's below the lowest tax bracket rate of 15 percent, so you may have to ask for

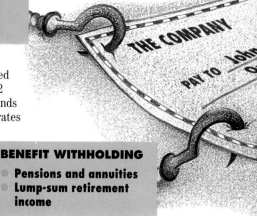

BENEFIT WITHHOLDING
- Pensions and annuities
- Lump-sum retirement income

more tax to be withheld to avoid a large tax bill on April 15. You can use a W-4P to adjust the withholding up or down.

LUMP-SUM DISTRIBUTIONS
You may get a lump-sum payment if you change jobs or retire, or if your employer ends a pension plan. If you get a pension-plan distribution, beware of a withholding-tax trap. To escape the mandatory 20 percent withholding tax, you must arrange in advance to roll over the lump-sum payment directly from your former plan to a new pension plan or an IRA without having the money pass through your own hands.

BACKUP WITHHOLDING
The IRS's relentless crusade against unreported income has led to what it calls **backup withholding** on certain payments of interest, dividends and other income reported on Form 1099. Income in this category includes rents, fees

for independent contractors, royalties, gambling winnings and the proceeds from the sale of stocks, bonds and mutual-fund shares.

To avoid problems with backup withholding, fill out Form W-9, "Request for Taxpayer Identification Number and Certification," when you open a bank account, and when you make an investment or start to receive certain income. On the W-9, you must show your Social Security number—what the IRS calls your **Taxpayer Identification Number,** or **TIN**—and certify that you aren't subject to backup withholding.

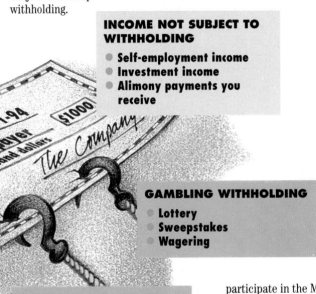

INCOME NOT SUBJECT TO WITHHOLDING
- Self-employment income
- Investment income
- Alimony payments you receive

GAMBLING WITHHOLDING
- Lottery
- Sweepstakes
- Wagering

BACKUP WITHHOLDING
- Interest payments
- Dividends
- Rental income
- Independent-contractor fees
- Royalties
- Proceeds from stock, bond and mutual-fund sales

If you give the wrong number or don't provide one, the payer may begin backup withholding at a rate of 31 percent, particularly on interest and dividends. The same can happen if the IRS says that you under-reported interest or dividend income on your latest tax return.

If you are notified that you listed an incorrect TIN, you can avoid backup withholding by sending your correct name and number to the payer. If you're accused of under-reporting interest or dividends, you must deal directly with the IRS. There are

severe penalties for giving false information to avoid backup withholding.

SOCIAL SECURITY AND MEDICARE
Withholding taxes are also used to finance Social Security and Medicare. The Social Security tax is 6.2 percent of your pay up to a ceiling that rises annually. In 1994, that ceiling was $60,600.

The Medicare tax is 1.45 percent of all your earned income. Under the **Federal Insurance Contributions Act (FICA),** your employer must contribute equal percentages to both Medicare and Social Security on your behalf.

Your employer takes care of reporting, collecting and paying its share of the withholding for these taxes. If you work for the federal government or another employer that isn't covered by the Social Security system, no money is withheld for Social Security. But you can choose to participate in the Medicare system and have the 1.45 percent withheld.

If you are self-employed, you must make estimated-tax payments during the year to cover both the employee's and the employer's contributions. The rates are 12.4 percent of all earnings, up to the pay ceiling of $60,600 for Social Security, and 2.9 percent for Medicare.

GAMBLING WINNINGS
If you are of a sporting mind, remember that gambling winnings of $5,000 or more are subject to a 28 percent withholding tax if they come from a sweepstakes, a betting pool or a lottery. This withholding also applies to any wager when the proceeds are at least 300 times the amount of the bet— unless the payoff is from bingo, keno or slot machines. A payer that withholds tax should send you Form W-2G, "Certain Gambling Winnings," showing the amounts won and withheld.

Estimated Taxes

Estimated taxes are the way to pay as you earn if you're self-employed or have a lot of investment income.

QUARTERLY ESTIMATED-TAX PAYMENT

WHO MUST PAY ESTIMATED TAXES?

You may have to pay estimated taxes up to four times a year if you fit any of these descriptions:

- You are self-employed—either full-time or part-time.

- You have a lot of investment income—including dividends, interest, rents, royalties or capital gains from selling securities or real estate.

- You receive unemployment benefits.

- You receive alimony payments.

- You win a big award, a lottery prize or a bet.

AVOIDING ESTIMATED TAXES ALTOGETHER

There is an escape hatch. You don't have to pay any estimated taxes if you satisfy both of these conditions:

- You had no tax liability for the prior full calender year, and

- You were a U.S. citizen or resident for that same entire year.

GETTING THE FORMS

You can get all tax forms and publications at an IRS office, or you can phone 800-829-3676 to order them. Once you have made your first estimated-tax payment, the IRS should mail you a set of 1040-ES forms with payment vouchers bearing your name, address and Social Security number.

DO YOU NEED TO PAY ESTIMATED TAXES?

Any income that isn't subject to withholding tax is subject to estimated-tax requirements. Even when tax is being withheld from your pay or other income, you must make estimated-tax payments if the withheld sums don't reach a certain minimum each quarter. The responsibility for seeing that the payments are made is yours.

Here is a test: If you meet both parts of it, you must make estimated-tax payments.

> **Projected tax bill**
> **− Withheld amounts**
> **− Projected credits**
> _____
> **= Additional tax owed**

PAY ESTIMATED TAX IF:

● Additional tax owed is over a certain amount ($500 for 1994) **and**

● Withholding and credits are less than:
  — 90% of current year's tax, or
  — 100% of previous year's tax (110% for some high-income taxpayers),

whichever is smaller.

Estimated taxes are periodic payments that you must make if you don't have enough withheld from your paychecks to cover a minimum amount of the taxes you'll owe by the end of the year. In 1992, almost 13 million Americans had to pay estimated taxes.

HOW TO ESTIMATE BY YOURSELF

Estimating tax payments is tricky. If you decide not to seek professional tax help, get started by having your latest tax return and IRS Form 1040-ES in front of you. This form provides instructions, a worksheet and four payment vouchers.

The 1040-ES instructions are skimpy. If you want to do the calculations yourself, get IRS Publication 505, "Tax Withholding and Estimated Tax," a 54-page booklet that provides detailed counsel covering the intricacies of self-employment taxes (which are actually payments to Social Security and Medicare), as well as capital gains and the limits on itemized deductions and personal exemptions.

The worksheets in Publication 505 ask you to estimate as closely as possible your anticipated adjusted gross income, standard or itemized deductions and exemptions for the year so you can come up with your expected taxable income.

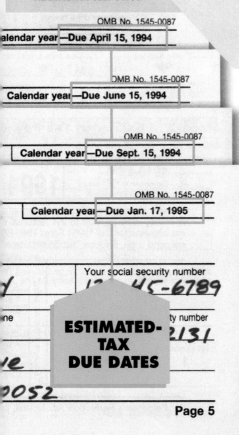

OMB No. 1545-0087

Calendar year —Due April 15, 1994

OMB No. 1545-0087

Calendar year —Due June 15, 1994

OMB No. 1545-0087

Calendar year —Due Sept. 15, 1994

OMB No. 1545-0087

Calendar year —Due Jan. 17, 1995

Your social security number
12? 45-6789

ty number
2131

0052

Page 5

ESTIMATED-TAX DUE DATES

HAUL IN THE FAMILY

Spouses with separate incomes should determine individually whether one or both should make estimated-tax payments, the IRS advises. Once a couple decides to make separate or joint estimated-tax payments, they can still decide later whether to file separate or joint tax returns.

If you file tax returns for children with significant investment income, you may need to make estimated-tax payments for them, too.

Estimated-Tax Strategies

The best advice: Avoid penalties. Don't fall behind on payments.

Once you've determined whether you have to pay estimated taxes, it's time to figure out how to best go about it.

PENALTY FOR LATE PAYMENT

APR 15   JUNE 15   SEPT 15   JAN 15

ESTIMATED TAX DUE

WHEN TO MAKE ESTIMATED PAYMENTS

The IRS divides the year into four unequal periods for estimated-tax purposes. The due dates are April 15, June 15, September 15 and January 15. Payments start on the due date for the period when you had taxable income. You may pay all you owe for the year on that date—or you can spread your payments over the remaining periods.

Most people start paying on April 15. The usual way is to divide the annual payment by four and send in equal amounts on each due date.

The good news is that you don't have to make an estimated-tax payment until you actually have the taxable income.

SIDESTEPPING THE PAYMENT TRAP

If you choose to pay in installments, beware of a nasty pitfall. If you don't pay enough on a due date, you may be charged an underpayment penalty—even though your total payments for the year later prove to exceed the tax you owe and you claim a refund when you file your return.

This trap may open if you start making payments after April 15—which generally is the first estimated-tax due date for the

DON'T OVERLOOK PAST PAYMENTS

All the tax payments you already have made may add up to an unexpected refund.

- When you file your tax return, be sure to take credit for all payments of withheld and estimated taxes.

- Take credit for withholding from sick pay, pensions, annuities and gambling winnings.

- Don't neglect backup withholding (see p. 44) from interest and dividends.

- Don't overlook excess withholding for Social Security. This can happen if you had more than one employer during the year and you earned more than $60,600.

year. You may also be vulnerable if your income, deductions or other vital factors change during the year.

The solution is to refigure your estimated tax if your tax situation changes. If you do, or if you make your first payment after April 15, you'll use the special worksheet in Publication 505 to determine the minimum amount to pay on each of the remaining due dates.

If your income isn't spread evenly through the year—for seasonal reasons, perhaps—you may make

Avoid penalties by weighing your tax burden as your financial situation changes.

one or more payments smaller than the amount figured with the regular method. See Publication 505 for the annualized-income method for calculating installments. If you adopt that method, though, you must add Form 2210, "Underpayment of Estimated Tax by Individuals and Fiduciaries," to your year-end return.

HOW TO MAKE ESTIMATED PAYMENTS

You have two options here. First, you may have already paid more taxes than you owe. You can have any excess tax payment for one year credited to your estimated tax for the following year. You apply this excess to your first estimated-tax payment instead of claiming a refund. There is a line on your tax return for doing this.

The other way to pay is simply to mail your check with the 1040-ES voucher. Keep a record of your payments.

ESTIMATED-TAX PENALTIES

If the combination of your withholding and estimated-tax payments doesn't reach an annual or an interim threshold, you may be penalized for underpayment of estimated tax.

Penalties are figured separately for each payment period. That means you may be penalized for a period even if you make up the shortfall later. That's why it is essential to refigure your estimated tax whenever your finances change.

Apply last year's overpayment to this year's estimated tax.

THIS YEAR **LAST YEAR**

Publication 505 explains how to figure the penalty yourself on Form 2210—and how to pay it. The IRS, however, concedes

that this is complicated and encourages you to let the IRS figure the penalty for you and send you a bill. If you go this route, you must first answer some questions on Form 2210. If any of a half-dozen items applies to you, you must complete the tax form and attach it to your return.

THE PENALTY RATE

The penalty for underpayment is charged from the date a payment was due to the date it is made. The rate is a percentage of the underpayment—and is variable. The IRS refigures the percentage quarterly, according to a formula. In 1994, it was set at an annual rate of seven percent during the first and second quarters, eight percent in the third, and nine percent in the fourth.

WAIVING PENALTIES

You could be penalized for underpaying for one payment period even if you make it up later in the year.

You may use Form 2210 to ask the IRS to waive an underpayment penalty. The IRS can be lenient if your failure to make a required payment stemmed from:

- A casualty or some other circumstance that would make a penalty unfair.
- A disability.

TAX-FORECASTING STRATEGIES

Forecasting your taxes so that you can nudge your payments over the right threshold may seem like so much guesswork. Here are some things to keep in mind:

- Paying 100 percent or 110 percent of the preceding year's tax is a safe solution.
- If you have a reasonable guess as to what you'll be making, consider paying 90 percent of the current year's estimated tax. Unless you have high income and a big jump in tax from a year before, this method should let you make smaller payments.
- If tax is being withheld from your salary, and you can see that you haven't paid enough estimated tax on other income, have your employer increase withholding for the rest of the year.
- In doing year-end tax planning, remember to figure the effect on your estimated tax for the following year.
- After you figure your estimated taxes due to Uncle Sam, get right to work on any state and local estimated taxes.

Who Must File

Whether you must file a tax return depends mainly on your income, your filing status and your age.

Baring your financial soul to the IRS every year can be an intimidating, even frightening, experience—but it doesn't have to be. Your return may be painless or elaborate, depending on the story you have to tell. Whatever the case, assembling all your financial records and reviewing them at least once a year can be enlightening. The process can help you get an idea of how much you spent last year, and how much money you'll need to make it through the coming year.

FOCUSING YOUR FINANCES

The tax return helps you focus on your income and expenses for the past year. First, it shows the money you

received from each source of income. Then you learn how much you laid out for taxes, medical bills and other major expenses.

The information you assemble can form the basis for creating a household budget, or for planning your family's financial future.

Too many people pass up this annual opportunity to take stock of their finances. Nearly half of all tax returns every year are done by paid tax preparers. If you are brave enough to do your own, or diligent enough to review the one you pay someone else to prepare, you'll be ready to set your financial course for the coming year.

Taxpayer Thresholds

You must file a return if your annual income is above the threshold amount for your **filing status** (see the chart below). The threshold amount is lowest if you're single, and rises if you're married, or if you're a head of a household or 65 or older.

Americans Abroad

American citizens living outside the U.S. follow the same filing requirements as U.S. citizens living in the states. That's because the U.S.—unlike most other countries—taxes the income of its citizens no matter where they earn it.

Americans living abroad, however, do not usually pay as much as Americans living at home. The theory is that the reduced taxes will be offset by taxes imposed by foreign countries. If you qualify, you can choose to exempt a large part of your overseas pay and some of your housing costs from U.S. taxation. Another option is to take a credit on your U.S. return for the income taxes you paid in the foreign country.

1994 FILING REQUIREMENT THRESHOLDS

You must file a tax return if your **gross income**, the total amount of your income from all sources, rises above the following amounts:

Filing Status	Gross Income Under Age 65	Gross Income Age 65 and Over
Single	$ 6,250	$ 7,200
Head of household	$ 8,050	$ 9,000
Married, filing a joint return	$11,250	$12,750*
Married, filing separate returns	$ 2,450	$ 2,450

* This figure applies if both spouses are 65 or older. If one spouse is under age 65 and the other is over 65, the threshold amount is $12,000.

Cut Out the Paperwork

Each year, about 1.5 million Americans, nearly half of them over the age of 65, don't need to file returns but do so anyway. An IRS study found that most of these people feared incorrectly that they would get in trouble with the IRS if they didn't file every year. Over a third of these returns were done by paid preparers—who should have known better. Others who didn't need to file deliberately had too much tax withheld from their pay only because they liked getting refunds. The IRS doesn't want to process pointless paperwork any more than you do, so read the filing requirements carefully.

Dependents

If you are someone's dependent—no matter what your age—you fall into a category with special rules. Dependents must be either relatives or full-time members of your household, and they must receive over half of their financial support from you. If the dependent is not your child—an elderly parent, for example—that person must report little or no gross income. (For 1994, the threshold was $2,450 in gross annual income.) Gross income in this case includes income from all sources, including rental income.

You must report the Social Security number of each of your dependents who is at least a year old.

Children With Income

If your child is under age 14 and has income from interest and dividends alone that totals less than $5,000, you can report that income on your own return. Your child doesn't have to file separately, but you need to file Form 8814.

Children don't have to file at all if they have no earned income (from salary or wages), and if the income they receive (from interest or dividends, for example) is less than $3,700. Children with both unearned and earned income don't have to file if the total falls below $600.

Refund Recipients

If you aren't required to file a return but still qualify for a tax refund or the earned-income credit (EIC) for low-income wage earners, you should file to get your money back.

THE DEPENDENCY TEST

A person who meets all of these conditions may be considered your dependent:

☑ **1.** Lives with you for the whole year, or is your near relative.

☑ **2.** Is a U.S. citizen or a resident of the U.S., Canada or Mexico.

☑ **3.** Doesn't file a joint return with anyone, except to get a refund.

☑ **4.** Has income less than $2,450 (for 1994), unless the person is your child and under age 19 (under 24, if a student).

☑ **5.** Receives over half of all their support from you. (Special rules apply to children of divorced or separated parents.)

Special rules also apply to people who share someone's support. For example, a sister and a brother who together provide over half the support for their invalid mother may be able to claim her as a dependent in alternate years. See Form 2120, "Multiple Support Declaration," for more information.

Finding Tax Information

Perhaps the best source—and certainly the cheapest—is the IRS itself.

The IRS offers a wealth of free taxpayer assistance, including some 120 publications on specific topics.

Its most important booklet is the comprehensive IRS Publication 17, "Your Federal Income Tax." It explains all of the important changes in tax law that may affect your return, and it has a helpful section that answers frequently asked tax questions. It's a must if you prepare your own return—and it's free.

You should also get Publication 553, "Highlights of Tax Changes," and the "Guide to Free Tax Services: Free Tax Help Every Season." You can get these publications by calling 1-800-829-3676 or by visiting the nearest IRS office.

Many libraries have IRS audio and video cassettes that tell you, step by step, how to prepare your own return. IRS offices also lend videotapes that explain personal and business taxes, audits and other tax matters. Some are in Spanish. Groups can borrow the tapes without charge.

Special IRS services are available to aid the deaf, the blind and Americans living abroad. The IRS has full-time staffers at 13 U.S. embassies around the world. See the "Guide to Free Tax Services" for more information.

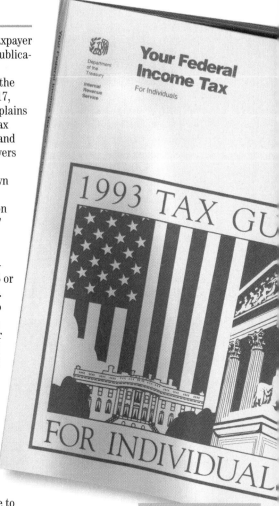

WALK-IN ASSISTANCE

Aides at IRS offices will help you do your return free of charge. In 1993, the aides helped seven million filers. However, the IRS doesn't have to take responsibility for an employee's mistake, unless it was made in formal written advice.

TOLL-FREE TELEPHONE AID

You can call a number shown in your tax package to talk to an IRS aide. More than 35 million filers used this service in 1993. But don't be surprised if it takes a while to work your way past the busy signals. A congressional agency, the General Accounting Office, graded the accuracy of IRS replies in 1994 at 89 percent.

TELE-TAX

This automated, toll-free phone system provides recorded information on 140 tax topics, some in Spanish. But it doesn't answer individual questions. You choose the topics you want to hear about from a recorded list.

Tele-Tax is open around the clock, every day. It received over 30 million calls in 1993. Your tax package lists Tele-Tax topics and the phone number to call.

Tele-Tax will also tell you when you'll receive your refund. This automated

IRS TOLL-FREE INFORMATION

Personal help line*
1-800-829-1040

To order forms
1-800-829-3676

Tele-Tax*
1-800-829-4477

Hearing impaired
1-800-829-4059

*in most areas

service is available on weekdays. Get out your return copy, call the Tele-Tax number and follow the recorded instructions. You'll be asked to enter some information, including the exact amount of your refund.

THE VOLUNTEER ARMY

The IRS trains nearly 100,000 volunteers from charitable groups who offer free help with returns to low-income taxpayers, the elderly, the disabled, taxpayers who don't speak English well and others with special needs. Volunteers help well over three million filers a year.

The programs are called Volunteer Income Tax Assistance (VITA) and Tax Counseling for the Elderly (TCE). Most of the local sponsors are units of the American Association of Retired Persons (AARP). The programs are held in community centers, community colleges, libraries, churches and shopping malls. IRS offices can tell you where.

Many law and accounting schools sponsor free tax clinics staffed by student volunteers who can represent taxpayers facing an audit.

TAX GUIDES

You can find line-by-line guidance to doing your return in fat volumes from J.K. Lasser, H&R Block, Ernst & Young, Consumer Reports and others. The information comes from IRS Publication 17. These volumes are updated annually and toss in some of the tax-saving tricks of the trade used by professional tax preparers.

Don't use the same tax guide you used last year. Because tax laws change, always use a current guide.

Plenty of books and periodicals offer tax-return preparation and tax-planning tips. *The Wall Street Journal, SmartMoney* magazine and similar publications offer many articles on these subjects.

TAX AND BOOKKEEPING SOFTWARE

Some financial software programs designed for home computers have a tax component in addition to their checkbook and other financial features. Other programs just help you fill out your tax return. The programs prompt you to enter your tax data and then do the computations. They also advise you on how to prevent common errors and point out tax savings you might have missed.

You'll have to spend time learning a program's conversational style and its quirks. If a tax point baffles you, software is no substitute for a professional tax adviser. Still, tax software can be helpful. Some people use it to help them get ready for a meeting with a tax preparer.

Tax programs let you print a return you can send to the IRS. The forms can be identical to the regular forms, or they can be in the concise form called 1040PC. (See p. 77.)

The popularity of tax software is soaring. Software publishers estimate that they sold more than 2.2 milli on programs that helped taxpayers file their 1993 federal returns. Among the best sellers are TurboTax by Intuit, TaxCut by MECA Software and Personal Tax Edge by Parsons Technology. You can get separate software to do the returns for some states.

Guide to
Free Tax Services

FREE TAX HELP EVERY SEASON
For tax year 1993

Publication 17
Cat. No. 10311G
For use in preparing 1993 returns

THE WALL STREET JOURNAL WEDNES

Tax Report

A Special Summary and Forecast Of Federal and State Tax Developments

PERSONAL EXEMPTIONS and other tax benefits will rise slightly for 1995.

These tax benefits are tied each year to the cost of living. Based on inflation data released yesterday, James C. Young, an assistant professor at George Mason University in Fairfax, Va., figures the personal exemption on returns for 1995 will rise to $2,500, up from $2,450 for 1994. The standard deduction for married couples filing jointly will rise $200 to $6,550; for singles, it will rise $100 to $3,900, according to his unofficial calculations. For married couples filing se

e 12
the
vas

Getting Professional Help

Skilled tax preparers save you time, aggravation and taxes. But remember: You, not the preparer, are responsible for your return.

Many taxpayers don't do their own returns because of the time and effort involved. Others are confused by the process or are afraid of the IRS. Still others have complex tax situations that require professional help.

To decide whether to do your own taxes or not, ask yourself a few questions: Can you file the simple Form 1040EZ, or must you file the more complicated Form 1040? (See p. 62 for more information on

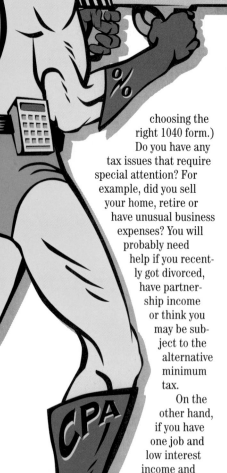

choosing the right 1040 form.) Do you have any tax issues that require special attention? For example, did you sell your home, retire or have unusual business expenses? You will probably need help if you recently got divorced, have partnership income or think you may be subject to the alternative minimum tax.

On the other hand, if you have one job and low interest income and choose to take the standard deduction instead of itemizing, you should have no problem doing your own taxes.

TAX PREPARERS

You will find a vast array of preparers with widely varying abilities to choose from. Their fees can vary, too. Their abilities aren't easy to judge, because there's no standardized test or license for tax preparers. Anyone can hang out a shingle and claim to be a tax expert.

Trained preparers include **commercial services, financial planners, enrolled agents** and **certified public accountants (CPAs)**.

Tax lawyers rarely prepare personal returns. They generally concentrate on giving tax advice and representing clients in tax disputes. Their hourly fees are high.

COMMERCIAL SERVICES

Commercial services range from big concerns, which train their employees, to individuals who may be self-taught. Firms such as H&R Block, Jackson Hewitt and Triple Check typically charge modest fees and prepare uncomplicated returns for middle-income clients. They can advise you at an audit, but they can't speak for you before the IRS.

ACCREDITED TAX PREPARERS AND ADVISERS

A more expensive approach is to hire a tax preparer with more credentials. One type is the accredited tax preparer, a title conferred by the Denver-based College for Financial Planning, not by a government agency. The college also created the designation of certified financial planner.

Accredited tax preparers and advisers cannot represent you in dealings with the IRS.

ASK YOUR PREPARER:

- What training and recent education in personal taxes has the preparer had?
- How many personal returns did the preparer do for the latest year?
- What experience does the preparer have with tax situations like yours?
- Is the preparer available year-round to handle questions and problems?
- Does the preparer interpret tax laws and regulations conservatively or aggressively?
- How much will your return cost to prepare?
- What experience has the preparer had in dealing directly with the IRS? What are the services and fees in case of an audit?

ENROLLED AGENTS

Enrolled agents have either worked for the IRS or passed a two-day IRS test for doing complex returns. They also must meet continuing education requirements. They can represent you at an audit and at other meetings with the IRS. If you anticipate having problems with the IRS, an enrolled agent may be well worth the price. They typically charge $100 to $300 to prepare a return.

CERTIFIED PUBLIC ACCOUNTANTS

All CPAs have passed state accountancy tests and must meet continuing education requirements. Typically, they do more complicated returns for professionals, executives and investors. CPAs can provide year-round accounting and tax services for the self-employed. However, many CPAs are not specialists in personal taxes.

CPAs can represent you during an audit. In general, they charge more than other preparers. A relatively simple return prepared by a CPA may cost $200 to $300. In major cities, CPAs' hourly rates can be $100 to $200—which means you can expect fees of $500 and up for a return.

CHOOSING THE RIGHT TAX PREPARER

The complexity of your return and your willingness to pay for help are two important factors in choosing a preparer. Be sure to pick someone who will be there after the return-filing season ends.

Personal compatibility may count in addition to competence. You may rest easier with a conservative, play-it-safe approach to deductions than with an aggressive one. Remember: You are responsible for your return, no matter who prepares it.

You can find preparers listed in advertisements and telephone directories. State and county societies of enrolled agents and CPAs can give you names of their members. Ask your relatives, friends and business associates for recommendations.

> H&R Block signs more than 24 percent of all returns done by tax preparers. Its offices get an average $58 to prepare a typical return and about $111 for their "executive service."

Collecting and Keeping Records

Knowing what records to keep, and for how long, can save you time—and lots of shoeboxes.

Every year, the IRS is inundated with well over one billion records of money changing hands. Several of those records concern your money. The records are sent by your employer and your bank, as well as by the companies you invest in. Even a record of your gambling winnings is sent in. The IRS enters the data into its computers and checks the information against the income you report on your return. If the numbers don't jibe, the IRS will ask for an explanation. That's why it's so important to keep all of these records on hand.

RECORDS TO KEEP

- **Cash donations**
- **Non-cash donations, such as works of art or used clothing**
- **Capital gains and losses**
- **Tax-free interest on state and local bonds**
- **Home-office expenses**
- **Self-employment income and expenses**
- **Withheld and estimated taxes already paid**
- **Interest paid on mortgages and home-equity loans**
- **Purchase price and improvement costs of a home**
- **Job-related expenses**
- **Tip income**
- **Transportation expenses for charitable services**
- **Casualty and theft losses**
- **Medical and dental expenses**
- **Alimony paid or received**
- **Value of gifts you receive**
- **Safe-deposit-box fees**
- **Purchase prices of uniforms and work tools**
- **Union dues**

KEEPING BOOKS ON A HOME

Homeowners should take special care to save the records that document the cost of buying and improving a home. You should also keep track of any casualty-losses you claim for damages to your home. These records will determine your capital gain or loss when you sell your home.

You must report the gain or loss from selling your home on IRS Form 2119, "Sale of Your Home." You must attach this form to your tax return even if you don't pay tax on any gain. For more information, see IRS Publication 523, "Selling Your Home," and page 102 of this guide.

PROOF OF PAYMENT

A canceled check alone isn't necessarily proof of what a payment was for. It's better to have dated and signed receipts, invoices, sales slips, credit-card statements and/or bank-account statements along with your canceled checks.

INSURANCE
LOSS STATEMENT

CHARITIES

DENTAL

PAPERWORK THAT COUNTS

The deductions you use to reduce your taxes come from records you must collect yourself.

Creating your own orderly paper trail will not only help you figure your deductions accurately, but will also save time during the tax season. And orderly records are indispensable if you get audited.

As a start, simply keep your tax-related documents in one place during the year. You'll be even further ahead of the game if you file documents for different kinds of income and expenses in separate envelopes. Your tax accountant will be thrilled if you keep a diary of major expenses and write clear notes in your checkbook to explain each payment and deposit. You will be considered a saint if you present your accountant with the totals for each category.

YOU SHOULD KEEP SOME RECORDS INDEFINITELY

The period of limitations provided by law is generally three years. That means that the IRS must audit you within three years after the date you file a return—or two years after you pay the tax, whichever is later. But the IRS gets six years if you underreport income by more than 25 percent—and it's open season forever on tax fraud.

You should keep all records for at least three years after filing the return. Some records, such as those for home ownership and improvement, should be kept indefinitely.

KEEP INDEFINITELY

- Copies of returns
- Records related to tax disputes
- Records of retirement-account contributions and withdrawals
- Investment records
- Records of home ownership and improvements

KEEP AT LEAST 7 YEARS

- W-2s, 1099s and 1098s
- Canceled checks and receipts
- Bank and stockbrokers' statements
- Other papers that show income or that support deductions

The W-2

The W-2 tells you—and the IRS—how much money you made on the job last year and how much was withheld in taxes.

The W-2 is the most important tax record for the vast majority of taxpayers. It comes in the mail from your employer in January, details your pay and withheld taxes, and must be attached to your return. For most taxpayers, it's the only record filed with the return.

Your employer makes as many as six copies of your W-2 if you pay state and local income taxes as well as federal tax. The employer forwards Copy A to the Social Security Administration, keeps Copy D and sends the rest of the copies to you.

You must file Copy B with your federal return, which gets sent to the IRS. Copy 1 goes with your state return, and Copy 2 with your local return. Be sure to keep Copy C with your own records.

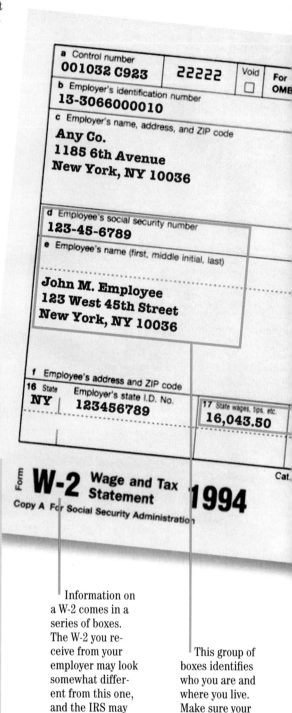

MAKE SURE THE INFORMATION IS CORRECT

Make sure the information on your W-2 is correct by checking the numbers against the year-end totals on your paycheck stub. Also make sure your name, address and Social Security number are correct. If there is a mistake, contact your employer immediately. If you don't get the mistake corrected by February 15, call the IRS toll-free number and be prepared to report the totals from your year-end paycheck stub.

Information on a W-2 comes in a series of boxes. The W-2 you receive from your employer may look somewhat different from this one, and the IRS may change the box numbers from year to year. But the basic information remains the same.

This group of boxes identifies who you are and where you live. Make sure your address is correct.

This group of boxes shows the wages, tips and other compensation that are subject to federal withholding. The figure in the box for wages, tips and other compensation may not be the same as in the box for Social Security wages. That's because the Social Security tax applies only to earned income up to a ceiling—$60,600 for 1994. There's no earned-income ceiling for the Medicare tax.

The wages figure does not include your yearly "pre-tax" contribution to a company pension plan or flexible-spending account.

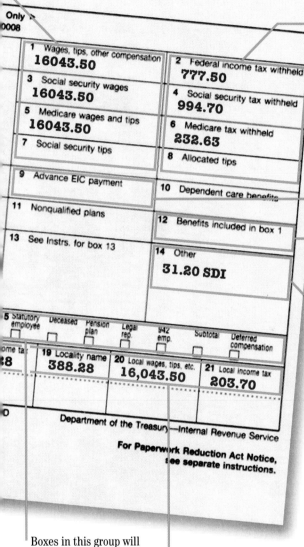

This group shows the total federal income taxes, Social Security taxes and Medicare taxes withheld by your employer for the year.

These boxes show earned-income credits paid in advance and dependent-care benefits paid to you, if any.

This shows the total value of perks—such as a company car—that your employer reported to the IRS. The total is included in your wages and salary reported in Box 1.

This box, mysteriously entitled "Other," shows the deductions for state disability insurance. If your state doesn't have such a plan, the box will be empty.

Boxes in this group will be checked if any of the categories apply to you—for example, if you belong to a pension plan or contributed to a company retirement plan such as a 401(k). Review this carefully. If the pension plan box is checked, you may not be allowed to take a tax deduction for an IRA contribution.

This group deals with the amount of income subject to withholding for state and local income taxes. If you itemize your deductions, the withheld amounts should be entered on Schedule A.

1099s

The IRS already knows a lot about you from the 1099s and other reports it receives with your name on them.

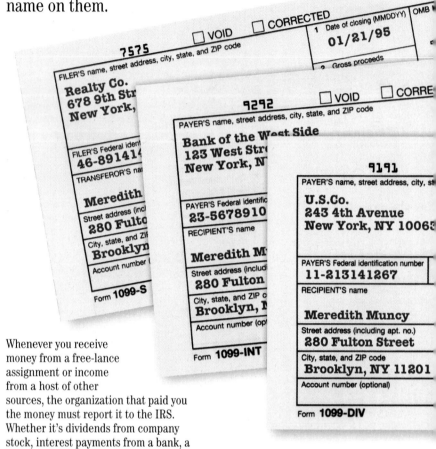

Whenever you receive money from a free-lance assignment or income from a host of other sources, the organization that paid you the money must report it to the IRS. Whether it's dividends from company stock, interest payments from a bank, a distribution from a pension fund or just about any income that is not your salary, the annual total is reported to you—and to the IRS—on a 1099 form.

The IRS has many kinds of information-reporting forms. Some report payments to you of rents, royalties or the proceeds of real-estate transactions. Form 1098, "Mortgage Interest Statement," is filed by a bank or someone who receives $600 or more in mortgage-interest payments from you.

Most of the more arcane boxes on your 1099s—such as fishing-boat proceeds on 1099-MISC—will be empty. The numbers that are filled in, however, go on your tax return.

One of the most common 1099s is the 1099-DIV, which reports stock and mutual-fund dividends. This form will tell you what part of your gross dividend income is taxable as **ordinary income** and

Partnerships are not taxable entities themselves. Instead, the income and losses from them are "passed through" to the personal returns of the owners—called partners. As a partner, you pay tax on your share of the partnership income, even on income that isn't paid out to you. General partners are personally liable for the business's debts and for each other's wrongful business acts. Limited partners, on the other hand, don't share in running the business and put only their investments, not their personal assets, at risk. Partnership income is reported to the IRS on a K-1 form.

Proceeds From Real Estate Transactions

(optional)   OMB No. 1545-0112

1994   Interest Income

☐ CORRECTED

	1a Gross dividends and other distributions on stock (Total of 1b, 1c, 1d, and 1e)	OMB No. 1545-0110	
ode	$ 807.69	**1994**	**Dividends and Distributions**
	1b Ordinary dividends		
	$ 807.69		
identification number	1c Capital gain distributions	2 Federal income tax withheld	**Copy A**
9234	$ 0.00	$ 0.00	For **Internal Revenue Service Center**
	1d Nontaxable distributions	3 Foreign tax paid	File with Form 1096.
	$	$ 0.00	For Paperwork Reduction Act Notice and instructions for completing this form, see **Instructions for Forms 1099, 1098, 5498, and W-2G.**
	1e Investment expenses	4 Foreign country or U.S. possession	
	$		
	Liquidation Distributions		
2nd TIN Not. ☐	5 Cash $	6 Noncash (Fair market value) $	

Cat. No. 14415N   Department of the Treasury - Internal Revenue Service

what part, if any, is taxable as **capital gain**. It will also show any payments that are tax-exempt.

THE 1099-MISC: INDEPENDENT CONTRACTORS

Form 1099-MISC reports your income as an independent contractor. The IRS says the classification is fraught with fraud. Many employers try to evade the costs of paying medical benefits and half of their workers' Social Security taxes by treating them as contractors instead of employees. And many employees try to avoid withholding taxes by claiming to be contractors.

The IRS runs a crusade against the misclassification of employees as independent contractors. If it sees that you have one main client who controls not only what you do but also how you do it, the IRS may classify you as an employee and penalize your employer for sending you a 1099-MISC instead of a W-2. If you're in doubt, ask the IRS about the tests for employee classification.

RECORDS AUTOMATICALLY PROVIDED TO THE IRS

Record	What It Reports
W-2	Employee pay and withheld taxes
W-2G	Gambling winnings
1098	Mortgage interest you paid
1099-B	Capital gains or barter proceeds
1099-DIV	Dividend income
1099-G	Unemployment pay or state tax refunds
1099-INT	Interest Income
1099-MISC	Income from rents, royalties or free-lance work
1099-R	Retirement-plan income
1099-S	Proceeds from real-estate transactions
K-1	Income from a partnership, S corporation or trust

Choosing the Right Tax Form

The 1040 comes in three flavors: the pared-down 1040EZ, the intermediate 1040A and the legendary 1040. The one to use depends on your filing status, your income and your deductions and credits. It makes sense to file the least-complicated return you can.

1040EZ

More than 17 million taxpayers, or 15 percent, got by with the 1040EZ in 1993.

People with simple finances can usually breeze through this one-page form.

The requirements for filing a 1040EZ are:

- **Under age 65 and not blind**

- **Single or married filing jointly with your spouse**

- **No dependents**

- **Taxable income under $50,000**

- **Taxable income only from wages, tips, scholarships and fellowships, and interest of no more than $400**

- **No itemized deductions, credits or adjustments (adjustments include IRA deductions and alimony paid—see p. 67)**

1040A

Well over 22 million taxpayers, or 20 percent, filed the 1040A.

The 1040A has no limits on age, filing status or dependents.

The requirements for filing a 1040A are:

- **Taxable income under $50,000**

- **No alimony paid or received**

- **No taxable state income-tax refunds**

- **No capital gains**

- **No rental income**

- **No self-employment income**

- **No itemized deductions or adjustments (except for IRAs)**

The 1040A may also be used by filers who have to pay the alternative minimum tax (AMT).

IT'S NOT EZ FOR EVERYONE

In general, taxpayers must fill out more paperwork if they want to qualify for a reduction in taxes. For example, blind taxpayers are not allowed to file a 1040EZ. Blind taxpayers, like taxpayers who are age 65 or older, qualify for different deductions from other taxpayers.

THE UN-SELF-RELIANT AMERICAN

Most of us would sooner repair our auto transmissions than prepare a tax return. The reason is simple: Even low-income taxpayers with relatively straightforward returns need help to figure complexities like the earned-income credit.

Who uses Paid Preparers?	
1040	72.0%
1040A	17.6%
1040EZ	3.5%

MARKING TIME

The IRS estimates that it takes the average taxpayer about ten-and-a-half hours to prepare a basic 1040 return from start to finish. And that's for people who don't itemize. The IRS estimates more time is needed for attachments and schedules, including 69 minutes to itemize deductions on Schedule A.

AVERAGE TIME IT TAKES TO DO A BASIC 1040

Record-keeping and studying rules		**5 hrs 55 mins**
Filling out the return	+	**3 hrs 44 mins**
Copying and mailing	+	**53 mins**
TOTAL TIME	=	**10 hrs 32 mins**

Nearly 70 million people, or not quite two-thirds of all taxpayers, used the long Form 1040.

The 65-line behemoth Form 1040 welcomes taxpayers with open arms—and plenty of appendages. Some 70 schedules and forms may be attached to the 1040 to cover every type of income, deduction and credit that must be reported.

You must file Form 1040 if you:

- **Have income above $50,000**
- **Are self-employed**
- **Have capital gains or losses**
- **Receive or pay alimony**
- **Itemize deductions**

WHAT'S IN A LABEL?

The IRS is eager for you to stick the mailing label on your return and enclose the forms in the bar-coded envelope that comes in your tax package. The bar codes speed processing and prevent errors when your return gets to the IRS. Don't worry about the code numbers you see. The IRS and many tax professionals insist the codes are only for routing your return and have nothing to do with picking you for an audit. The bar codes are explained in your tax package instructions.

SE HABLA ESPAÑOL

Some basic tax forms and publications are available in Spanish. Some of the Spanish forms are specifically designed for residents of Puerto Rico. Call 1-800-829-3676 and wait for the Spanish instructions. The IRS's Tele-Tax toll-free phone service—1-800-829-4477—also offers recorded tax information in Spanish.

HOW TO GET THE FORMS

If you filed a return by yourself last tax season, the IRS will send you the current forms for the next round in January. If a paid preparer signed your previous return, however, the IRS saves money by mailing you a postcard instead. Take this card to your preparer or use it to order forms for yourself.

Standard forms are available from IRS offices. During the spring filing season, you can find them in most post offices, banks, municipal centers and public libraries.

You can get IRS forms and other helpful tax publications by calling

1-800-829-3676.

Ask for the latest version of IRS Publication 17, "Your Federal Income Tax," while you're at it.

Using the 1040

Don't be squeamish about this form. It pays to dive in and understand the process of figuring your tax, even if someone else does it for you.

First, lay out your records to match the headings in the left-hand column of your 1040 return, namely **income, adjustments, deductions, tax computation** and **credits**. The instructions in the tax package will guide you through the return, line by line.

START AT THE TOP

Your identification label, which is mailed to the address you used the previous year, goes at the top of your return. Correct any errors on the label, and be sure to place the right label on the right form. A common mistake is attaching your state return label to the IRS return. If you have no label, print the information clearly.

FILING STATUS

Filing status plays a big role in determining your tax. A single person, for example, pays more tax than a married couple filing a joint return who have the same amount of taxable income. On the same taxable income, a single person will also pay more tax than an unmarried person who qualifies as a **head of household** making a home for others.

Couples who both have jobs may have to figure their taxes both jointly and separately to see which way saves them money. For help beyond the 1040 instructions, refer to IRS Publication 17, "Your Federal Income Tax."

THE IRS WILL FIGURE YOUR TAX FOR YOU

If it all seems too overwhelming, there's help. If you file a simple return by April 15, you can fill in the lines that apply to you and let the IRS figure your refund or tax payment. You won't owe interest or a late-payment penalty if you pay the bill within 30 days after the IRS sends it,

or by April 15, whichever is later. And you may change your mind later by filing an amended 1040X return.

The IRS will figure the tax on any 1040EZ, but it sets conditions for a 1040A or a 1040. For example, a 1040 filer must have taxable income below $100,000 and may not itemize deductions.

START AT THE TOP AND GO LINE BY LINE Use the IRS instructions and worksheets as needed.

RETURN TO THE 1040 AND CONTINUE LINE BY LINE When you've completed your return, attach the required schedules and requested income records, such as the W-2.

PENNY WISE

The IRS is exacting, but not to the penny. You are allowed to round off all entries by dropping amounts under 50 cents and adding a dollar for an amount of 50 cents or more. This saves time and simplifies your calculations.

DETOUR TO THE TAX SCHEDULES AS REQUIRED
Enter the income or loss from the schedules on the appropriate line of your 1040.

HAIL TO THE CHIEF

By checking "Yes" on your return, you put $3 of your tax into the Presidential Election Campaign Fund. This helps finance the campaigns of candidates who have a minimum level of voter support. Your checkmark doesn't change your tax or your refund. Support for federal aid to presidential campaigns has dwindled. Fewer than 20 percent of the returns filed in 1994 had checkmarks in the "Yes" box.

Schedule A — **Itemized deductions** are listed on Schedule A. Homeowners can deduct mortgage-interest payments and property taxes here. This is also the place to deduct state and local income taxes, medical expenses, job-related expenses and charitable donations.

Schedule B — **Interest** and **dividends** are reported on the 1099 forms you receive in the mail. All investment income must be included in your gross income. If your dividend or interest income totals more than $400, use Schedule B.

Schedule C — If you're self-employed as a sole proprietor, you'll have to fill out Schedule C or C-EZ to report your **business income**. You'll also need to file Schedule SE, explained below.

Schedule D — You report the income you receive from selling property or corporate stock on Schedule D. This includes all of your **capital gains** and **losses**. See Publication 544, "Sales and Other Dispositions of Assets," and Publication 550, "Investment Income and Expenses," for more detailed explanations of Schedule D.

Schedule E — If you're in business as a **partner** or a **shareholder** in an S corporation, you report the income on Schedule E. This schedule is also used to report income from rental real estate, royalties, estates, trusts and real-estate-mortgage investment conduits (REMICs).

Schedule F — If you are a self-employed **farmer**, use Schedule F. Like sole proprietors, farmers may have to attach Schedule SE, explained below.

Schedule R — Schedule R is for computing credits for the **elderly** or **disabled**. This credit is available if your income falls below certain thresholds.

Schedule SE — If you are **self-employed**, you may have to attach Schedule SE, "Self-Employment Tax," to figure Social Security and Medicare taxes on your business income.

Schedule EIC — Information to support the **earned-income credit** designed to help low-income workers is reported on Schedule EIC.

Taxable Income Isn't Gross

You don't pay tax on the total, or "gross," income you earn—only on the part the tax code says is taxable.

What's Taxable...and What's Not

TAXABLE INCOME

- Earned income (wages, salaries, tips and some fringe benefits)
- Unearned income (interest, dividends and capital gains)
- Self-employment income
- Partnership income
- Real-estate rental income
- Royalty, estate and trust income
- Alimony income
- Pension income
- IRA income
- Unemployment and sick pay
- Strike benefits
- Gambling winnings
- Prizes, awards and cash payments for services
- Barter income
- Illegal income

INCOME THAT MAY BE TAXABLE

- Social Security benefits (taxable if your other income is substantial)
- State and local income-tax refunds (taxable if you deducted them in a previous year)

TAX-FREE INCOME YOU MUST SHOW ON YOUR RETURN

- Tax-exempt interest from state and local bonds

TAX-FREE INCOME YOU DON'T NEED TO REPORT

- Welfare, veterans' disability and workers' compensation benefits
- Supplemental security income (SSI) from Social Security
- Child support
- Gifts and inheritances
- Life-insurance proceeds received after a death
- Scholarships for tuition, if you are studying for a degree

IF BETTY BARTERS A BIT OF BUTTER...

When you barter, you trade something or perform a service in exchange for something or a service from someone else. No money changes hands, but legally you must report as income the value of whatever you got in the exchange.

TIPS ON TIPS

Tips are taxable. You need to pay estimated taxes on tips if your employer doesn't withhold taxes on them.

Every service worker knows that it isn't easy to predict tip income. You can keep daily records of your tips for a while and then project that income over the full year. Or you can base your estimate on the previous year's income.

This is what can happen if you don't keep good records: Judy, a bartender at a casino, wasn't keeping a record of her tips. When the IRS did an analysis of overall tipping at the casino, she couldn't disprove their findings and had to pay taxes based on the IRS estimate.

But when the IRS made a similar estimate for the following year, Judy was ready. She produced a diary in which she had written down her tips for each week. Even though the total of her tips turned out to be half of what the IRS had estimated, a U.S. Tax Court judge ruled that Judy's diary was more believable than the IRS's estimate—and she won her case.

ADJUSTMENTS

Take a quick look at Form 1040, and you'll see "Adjustments to Income." **Adjustments** are special deductions that reduce your gross income. They aren't subject to the limitations imposed on some itemized deductions.

The main adjustments are for IRAs, retirement plans for the self-employed and alimony paid. Beginning in 1994, qualified moving expenses are also deductible as an adjustment.

THE MAIN ADJUSTMENTS ARE:

- **Qualifying contributions to IRAs**
- **Half of the self-employment tax**
- **Contributions to Keogh and SEP retirement plans for the self-employed**
- **Alimony payments**
- **Qualified moving expenses**

FROM GROSS INCOME TO TAX OWED

Gross Income
– Adjustments
= **ADJUSTED GROSS INCOME**

Adjusted Gross Income
– Exemptions and Deductions
= **TAXABLE INCOME**

Tax on Taxable Income
– Credits
+ Other Taxes
= **TOTAL TAX**

Total Tax
– Withheld and Estimated-Tax Payments
= **REFUND OR PAYMENT DUE**

ADJUSTED GROSS INCOME

The number at the bottom of the first page of the 1040—**adjusted gross income**, or **AGI**—is the heart of your return. AGI is used to set the limits on exemptions, IRA contributions and itemized deductions. For example, if your AGI is over a certain amount, you may be required to use a worksheet in the instructions to figure the exemptions for yourself, your spouse and your dependents.

EXEMPTIONS

An **exemption** is a deduction you can take for yourself, a spouse and each dependent. Each exemption lets you subtract a set amount from your taxable income. The amount for one exemption—$2,450 in 1994—is **indexed**, or tied to the inflation rate, and usually rises every year.

The benefit of exemptions, however, is phased out if your AGI (adjusted gross income) rises above a set level, which is also indexed each year for inflation. The levels in 1994 for the phase-out are $111,800 for a single taxpayer and $167,700 for a couple filing jointly.

UNEMPLOYMENT COMPENSATION

Unfortunately, if you lose your job, there's no tax-deferred silver lining. Unemployment income is fully taxable. By January 31, you should receive Form 1099-G, which reports how much unemployment compensation you received in the prior year. Be sure to save enough to pay the tax. You may also have to make estimated-tax payments on it.

To Itemize or Not to Itemize?

As itemized deductions are whittled away by Congress, more taxpayers are opting for the standard deduction.

Every taxpayer is allowed to take a fixed **standard deduction**. The standard deduction amounts vary according to filing status and other factors, and are increased each year for inflation. If you can pile up your itemized deductions so that their total exceeds your standard deduction, you'll save money by itemizing.

In an effort to simplify record-keeping and tax preparation, the 1986 tax act increased the standard deduction and took away or limited many itemized deductions. For example, it eliminated the deductions for personal interest—including credit-card interest—as well as the deduction for state sales taxes. It also limited deductions for medical costs, casualty and theft losses and miscellaneous job-related expenses. The effects were to take millions of low-income people off the tax rolls and to increase the use of the standard deduction.

The amount of itemized deductions you can use is reduced if your adjusted gross income—or AGI— is above a threshold. Like the standard deduction, that amount is indexed each year for inflation. In 1994, the threshold was $111,800. If your AGI is above this amount, you may save on taxes by taking the standard deduction. A worksheet in the 1040 instructions will help you figure out what's best for you.

> **73 percent of all taxpayers took the standard deduction for 1992—and the numbers are growing.**

Schedule A—Itemized Deductions

(Schedule B is on back)

▶ Attach to Form 1040. ▶ See Instructions for Schedules A and B (Form 1040).

USE THE STANDARD DEDUCTION

IF Your total itemized deductions are *less* than the standard deduction, which in 1994 was:

For a single $3,800

For a couple filing jointly $6,350

For a head of household $5,600

The standard deduction increases if you or your spouse is age 65 or older, or blind.

ITEMIZE YOUR DEDUCTIONS

IF You have large deductible expenses. The four main categories are:

- State income and property taxes
- Home-mortgage interest
- Charitable contributions
- Medical expenses

FEAR OF DEDUCTIONS

Honest taxpayers sometimes hesitate to take legitimate deductions for fear that they may trigger an audit. You should take all the deductions you are entitled to. Just be sure to keep the canceled checks, receipts and other records that substantiate your claims. If you think a deduction looks out of place on your return, you may attach an explanation and copies of the supporting documents (never send original documents).

The more you understand the tax law and your rights, the more confidence you'll have in your deductions.

CHARTING THE AVERAGES

This chart lists the unofficial averages for four key itemized deductions reported on federal tax returns for 1992. There is, of course, no guarantee that the IRS will accept them as a rule of thumb. But averages are useful if you're wondering how your deductions compare with those taken by people in your income range. The averages are based on data from returns grouped by adjusted gross income, or AGI.

Adjusted Gross income	State and Local taxes	Interest Payments	Charity	Medical and Dental
$30–40,000	2,621	5,523	1,434	3,531
$40–50,000	3,230	5,974	1,462	3,472
$50–75,000	4,335	7,005	1,745	3,903
$75–100,000	6,211	8,776	2,298	6,422
$100–200,000	9,819	12,606	3,471	11,452
$200–500,000	21,984	19,862	7,613	36,085
$500–1,000,000	51,018	30,245	17,996	59,350
$1,000,000+	165,985	64,354	83,429	81,295

Source: Research Institute of America

STATE AND LOCAL TAXES

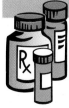

You may deduct income and real-estate taxes you pay to your state and local governments. You also may deduct the annual personal-property taxes that some states levy on the value of items such as a car (this doesn't mean sales taxes). Don't forget to deduct payments to state disability and unemployment funds that were withheld from your pay.

You can't deduct sales taxes, inheritance taxes, driver's license fees or garbage-collection fees.

INTEREST PAYMENTS

You may deduct interest on **home mortgages**, **home-equity loans** and money borrowed for investment or business purposes.

Other interest expenses aren't deductible. Mortgage-interest payments that you made are reported by the recipient to both you and the IRS on Form 1098.

You can't deduct interest payments made on behalf of someone else unless you, too, are legally responsible for the debt.

CHARITABLE CONTRIBUTIONS

You may deduct gifts to qualified religious organizations, schools, hospitals and other non-profit organizations.

If part of your gift pays for something you get that has more than a token value—such as a dinner or a concert—that portion of the gift is not deductible. It's up to the organization to tell you what the non-deductible amount of your gift is. For gifts of $250 or more, the charitable organization must give you a receipt for your gift. A canceled check by itself is not sufficient evidence.

If your donations exceed 20 percent of your adjusted gross income in a year, your deduction for that year may be limited.

MEDICAL AND DENTAL COSTS

Few people spend enough out of their own pockets on doctors, dentists and hospital bills to use this deduction these days.

For one thing, you can't deduct any payments for which you were reimbursed by insurance. The tax law lets you deduct only the amount of your total unreimbursed expenses that exceeds 7.5 percent of your adjusted gross income.

In adding up expenses to see if you cross that threshold, you may include health-insurance premiums you paid yourself and the costs of transportation to get to medical care.

Tougher Deductions

Not all deductions are created equal. Casualty, theft and miscellaneous deductions are hard to qualify for.

CASUALTY AND THEFT LOSSES

A casualty is damage to a car, home or other kinds of property, caused by a sudden, unexpected or unusual event or disaster. Fires, floods, earthquakes, tornadoes, accidents and vandalism are such events.

To deduct a casualty or theft loss, you must meet strict requirements and produce good records. You must show what happened and when. You have to prove the value of the damaged or stolen property, which may be much less than the price you paid for it.

If the property is insured, you must file an insurance claim if you hope to deduct a loss. Any insurance payment you receive reduces the amount you can deduct. A theft must have been reported to the police.

Even if you do have uninsured theft or casualty losses that qualify for a deduction, you still face severe limits on the amount you may deduct. First, you must subtract $100 from each loss. Then you must total your losses and subtract 10 percent of your AGI from the total. What's left, if anything, is your deduction.

For more about the amount and timing of these deductions, see Form 4684, Publication 17 and Publication 547, "Non-Business Disasters, Casualties and Thefts."

COMPUTING A CASUALTY OR THEFT-LOSS DEDUCTION: HOW IT WORKS

Let's say your uninsured car, valued at $5,000, is stolen. First, you subtract $100. Then you subtract 10 percent of your AGI. In this example, if your AGI is $49,000 or more, you can't deduct anything. But if your AGI is $40,000, here's what you can deduct:

Amount of Loss		$ 5,000
Subtract $100	–	100
		$ 4,900
Subtract 10% of your AGI	–	4,000
AMOUNT OF LOSS YOU CAN DEDUCT		**$ 900**

Tips on Casualty Losses

- A car accident isn't a casualty if your willful negligence caused it.

- Accidental breakage of china while you're washing it isn't a casualty.

- You can't claim a casualty loss from steady deterioration caused by such things as termites, drought, tree diseases or normal aging and weathering.

- If the U.S. president declares your area a federal disaster area, you get special treatment. See Publication 547.

HOME-OFFICE DEDUCTIONS

You can deduct expenses for business use of your home, including such costs as a home computer. But there are strict conditions and record-keeping rules. It is up to you to prove that the equipment and the space used to house that equipment are used only for business purposes. See Publication 587, "Business Use of Your Home," for more details.

Your home office doesn't need to fill a whole room. But it must be a separate space that is used exclusively and regularly as your main place of business, or as a place where you routinely meet clients, customers or patients. It may be a separate structure, such as a garage converted to office or storage space. (There are special rules for licensed day-care providers.)

If you use your home office while you're someone's employee, you must show you do it for the convenience of your employer and not just because it helps you in your job. This test is tough. You need a written statement from your employer.

Whether you use your home office as someone's employee or for your own business, the deduction for its expenses is limited. For one thing, if you're self-employed, you can't use home-office expenses to create a business loss that would enable you to avoid tax on other income.

MEALS, TRAVEL, ENTERTAINMENT AND OTHER MISCELLANEOUS EXPENSES

You may deduct car, travel and other kinds of job expenses that your employer doesn't pay for. You may also deduct the costs of producing or protecting income. But the severe restrictions on these miscellaneous deductions limit their value to many taxpayers. After totaling your miscellaneous items, you must then subtract 2 percent of your AGI. You get to deduct only the remainder.

Even so, it pays to keep records of unreimbursed business expenses. Meals and entertainment with clients are a major category here. The 1993 tax act reduced the meal and entertainment deduction from 80 percent to 50 percent of the actual cost.

Employee business expenses are reported on Form 2106. For more about these expenses, see Publication 17 and Publication 535, "Business Expenses." Other helpful publications are Publication 917, "Business Use of a Car," Publication 463, "Travel, Entertainment and Gift Expenses" and Publication 529, "Miscellaneous Deductions."

NEW RULES FOR MOVING

Starting in 1994, the cost of moving at least 50 miles to a new home because of a change of job or job location is treated as an adjustment instead of an itemized deduction. See Form 3903, "Moving Expenses," and Publication 17 or Publication 521, "Moving Expenses."

FORM 3903

HOBBY LOSSES

If you show losses from a sideline business in three out of five straight years, the IRS may think you're using losses from a pleasure-producing hobby to reduce the tax on your other income. It isn't illegal to enjoy your work or to show a string of losses. Still, you face back taxes, interest and penalties if you deduct losses but can't show a profit motive. The Tax Court ruled for the IRS in the recent cases of a rich lawyer who deducted $2.3 million in losses from raising polo ponies and an auto-body shop manager who deducted losses from tournament fishing.

To prove you have a profit motive, you must work in a businesslike manner—which means keeping books and records. You may deduct the expenses of a hobby-like activity, but no more than the income you receive from it. You must report the expenses as miscellaneous items, which are subject to the deduction limit. See IRS Publication 535.

EDUCATION

You may take a miscellaneous deduction for your own spending on education—but only if that education is required by your employer or the law to keep your present job or to maintain or improve skills needed in it. You can't deduct the expense of courses needed to meet the minimum qualifications of your present job. Nor can you deduct courses that prepare you for a different kind of work.

Getting to the Bottom Line

Now it's time to crunch the numbers to find out whether you'll get a refund or pay more tax.

Adjusted gross income minus deductions and exemptions equals taxable income. You figure your tax on that.

TAX TABLES

Tax tables calculate your tax according to your taxable income and your filing status.

TAX-RATE SCHEDULES

The four schedules—one for each filing status—apply to taxable income of $100,000 or more. A schedule shows how much tax you owe on most of your income. But you yourself calculate the tax on your top-bracket income and then your total tax.

CREDITS

After you compute the tax on your taxable income, you can whittle the number down even further with **tax credits**. Like deductions, credits reduce the amount of money you pay to the IRS. But unlike deductions and adjustments, credits show you just how much you save. A $100 deduction, for example, saves only the amount produced when you multiply $100 by your tax rate. Some deductions must also be above certain thresholds to save you money. A $100 credit, on the other hand, is subtracted directly from the tax you must pay.

Credits are Congress's attempt to be fair to taxpayers and to help those in difficult financial situations. The **foreign tax credit** is designed to be fair to Americans abroad who pay taxes to foreign countries. The **earned-income credit** is meant to help the working poor.

HERE ARE THE MAIN CREDITS:

- **Costs of child care and dependent care while you work (see Form 2441)**
- **Credit for the elderly or disabled with low incomes (see Schedule R)**
- **Credit for income taxes paid to foreign countries (see Form 1116)**
- **Earned-income credit for low-income taxpayers**

1994 Tax Table

If line 37 (taxable income) is—		And you are—			
At least	But less than	Single	Married filing jointly	Married filing separately	Head of a household
		Your tax is—			
59,000					
59,000	59,050	13,687	11,587	14,450	12,56
59,050	59,100	13,703	11,601	14,466	12,57
59,100	59,150	13,718	11,615	14,481	12,59
59,150	59,200	13,734	11,629	14,497	12,60
59,200	59,250	13,749	11,643	14,512	12,61
59,250	59,300	13,765	11,657	14,528	12,63
59,300	59,350	13,780	11,671	14,543	12,64
59,350	5				,66
59,400	5				67
59,450	5				
59,500	5				
59,550	5				
59,600	5				
59,650	5				
59,700	5				
59,75					

TAX TABLES: HOW THEY WORK

If you are married, filing jointly and have a taxable income of $59,000, you owe $11,587 in taxes.

OTHER TAXES

Sandwiched between the credits and the payments sections of Form 1040 is a section called *Other Taxes*. This grab bag includes the self-employment tax, the alternative minimum tax, and Social Security taxes and Medicare taxes on tips that weren't reported to your employer. It also includes advance earned-income-credit payments that you received in your paycheck. Add the total from this section to the tax figured above to find your total tax.

TAKING CREDIT FOR TAX PAYMENTS

When your final tax is computed, be sure to take the credits due for all your withheld and estimated taxes and any other payments you have made already. Include here any overpayments of Social Security taxes.

EARNED-INCOME CREDIT

If you are a worker with at least one child, and you earn less than a specified amount ($23,760 in 1994), you can have money in the form of the earned-income credit added to your paychecks. If the credit surpasses the tax you owe for the year, you will receive a refund. The largest possible EIC refund in 1994 was $2,364. To get the credit, ask your employer for Form W-5, "Earned Income Credit Advance Payment Certificate," or claim the credit on your return.

REFUND OR PAYMENT DUE

Compare your total payments—mostly withheld taxes and estimated-tax payments—with your total tax to see if you're getting a refund or paying more tax.

If you're getting a refund and you expect to pay estimated taxes for the current year, you may choose to apply part or all of the refund toward the estimated taxes.

Finally: Before you lick the envelope, check your math. Attach your W-2s, schedules and your check or money order—unless you're due for a refund. Be sure to put your Social Security number and the tax year on your check. Enter your occupation and sign and date the return. Be sure to make a copy for yourself before you mail it.

TAX-RATE SCHEDULES: HOW THEY WORK

If you are married, filing jointly and have a taxable income of

	$ 120,000
–	91,850
=	28,150
x	.31
=	8,727
+	20,778
YOUR TAX IS = $	**29,505**

Schedule X—Use if your filing status is **Sing**

If the amount on Form 1040, line 37, is:
Over— / But not over—

Schedule Z—Use if your filing status is **Head o**

If the amount on Form 1040, line 37, is:
Over— / But not over—

Schedule Y-2—Use if your filing status is **Married filing separately**

If the amount on Form 1040, line 37, is:
Over— / But not over—
Enter on Form 1040, line 38
of the amount over—

Schedule Y-1—Use if your filing status is **Married filing jointly or Qualifying widow(er)**

If the amount on Form 1040, line 37, is: Over—	But not over—	Enter on Form 1040, line 38	of the amount over—
$0	$38,000	.... 15%	$0
38,000	91,850	$5,700.00 + 28%	38,000
91,850	140,000	20,778.00 + 31%	91,850
140,000	250,000	35,704.50 + 36%	140,000
250,000	....	75,304.50 + 39.6%	250,000

WHAT IF YOU'VE MADE A MISTAKE?

You can file an amended return on Form 1040X. Use it to correct errors or make changes in income, deductions or credits on the return you filed. You should file the 1040X within three years after the original return was filed, or within two years after the tax was paid, whichever is later. If you don't, you may not qualify for any of the refund you claim. And don't forget that you may need to fix your state and local tax returns, too.

Paying Up

Midnight, April 15 is the witching hour, although extensions are automatic. But be careful. Extensions can be costly.

The rush to get returns postmarked before midnight on April 15 is legendary. Many post offices stay open right up to that fateful hour to accommodate procrastinators. But don't try any fancy stuff: Private postage-meter stamps don't count.

If April 15 falls on a weekend, the deadline is put off until the following Monday. If it falls on a legal holiday, the deadline moves to the next weekday.

If you miss the deadline, you'll be subject to penalties for filing late or paying late—or both.

Dear Bob—
Remember last year?
Let's pay our taxes on time and
AVOID PENALTIES AND INTEREST!
—Alice

PAYMENT OPTION 1

Pay by April 15

- **No penalty**
- **No interest**

Paying up in full is clearly the way to go. If you steadily put aside enough money during the year to cover your anticipated tax liability, you'll save money in the long run.

IT PAYS TO KEEP IN TOUCH

You can run, but you can't hide. If the IRS doesn't know where to reach you, you may pay a lot in interest and penalties when it does catch up with you. Say it sends a notice to your old address, telling you to explain something on your return or to drop in for an audit. You may be blissfully ignorant if the notice is delayed or lost. But if you do owe more tax, the interest and any penalties that may apply are mounting up all the time.

Try an ounce of prevention: Get Form 8822, "Change of Address," and send it to the IRS service center where you filed your latest return. That way, you will continue to receive tax-return packages and, most important, IRS notices that require a prompt reply.

PAYMENT OPTION 2

Pay by April 15 with an Extension

- **No penalty or interest, if estimated payment is correct**

If you need more time to file your return, you can get an automatic four-month extension by filing Form 4868, "Application for Automatic Extension of Time to File U.S. Individual Income Tax Return." Form 4868 must be mailed by April 15 and will give you until August 15 to file your return.

The form delays the deadline for filing your return—but not for paying tax. If you want to avoid interest and a late-payment penalty when you get a filing extension, you must estimate what you still owe and pay it by April 15, along with Form 4868.

To avoid a late-payment penalty, the amount of your check must be enough to bring your total payments to at least 90% of your actual tax bill. You'll still pay interest on the difference between what you've paid and what you owe. Interest and penalties start running on April 16 and accumulate until you pay.

YOU SIGN IT, YOU OWN IT

Signing your return is like taking a silent oath. It is the same as swearing in court, under a penalty of perjury, that the return is correct. After you sign, the burden of proof is on you in any dispute with the IRS.

In some situations, you may sign a return for your spouse or child, or you may sign as the representative of someone who died. In these cases, you must attach an explanation to the return.

If you pay someone to do your return, the preparer must sign it, too. But don't be fooled.

Sign Here
Keep a copy of this return for your records.

Under penalties of perjury, I declare that I have examined this return and accompanying schedules belief, they are true, correct, and complete. Declaration of preparer (other than taxpayer) is based

Your signature *John Q. Taxpayer*   Date *4/15/94*
Spouse's signature. If a joint return, BOTH must sign.   Date

Bob at the Post Office 4/15/94 11 PM

You are still responsible for the accuracy of every item on your return. If there's a discrepancy, you will pay the penalty, not the preparer.

INTEREST AND PENALTIES

The interest charged on overdue taxes is based on a market rate that is recalculated every quarter. The annual rate was 7 percent in the first two quarters of 1994, 8 percent in the third and 9 percent in the fourth. The actual charge is more than that because the interest is compounded daily.

The additional penalty for late payment is 0.5 percent of your unpaid balance per month—up to a maximum of 25 percent.

The penalty for filing your return late is generally 5 percent a month of the balance due, up to a maximum of 25 percent. However, this charge is reduced by the amount of the late-payment penalty.

PAYMENT OPTION 3

Pay after April 15

- **Penalty and interest until you pay**
- **Filing extensions available**

If you just don't have the money to pay up on April 15, the IRS urges you to request an extension and pay as much as you can at the time. That will cut down on the interest and late-payment penalty you'll have to pay later. If you need a filing extension, you can still request one with your partial payment.

If you aren't ready to file your return by August 15, you can request a two-month extension of the filing deadline by sending in Form 2688. But this time, you have to give a reasonable cause and obtain IRS approval. Interest and penalties continue to pile up if you don't pay.

Filing for extensions will not, as rumor has it, increase your chance of being audited. The best advice is to go ahead and get an extension if you need the extra time to file, but avoid this situation if you can.

PAYMENT OPTION 4

Pay after April 15 in Installments

- **Penalty and interest until you pay in full**
- **IRS must approve**

You can ask to pay all or some portion of what you owe in monthly installments by attaching Form 9465, "Installment Agreement Request," to your return. The IRS should tell you within 30 days whether it will grant your request. If you choose the installment route, you'll pay interest and a penalty to the IRS for the amount you don't pay—so it might be cheaper in the long term to borrow the money to pay your tax in full and avoid the installment plan altogether.

The IRS doesn't publish guidelines on how fast you must pay off overdue taxes in installments. Tax advisors suggest that you complete the payments within two years. For example, the IRS might agree to accept $100 a month for 18 months to settle a bill of $1,800 in taxes, interest and penalties.

IF YOU OWE A LOT

If you owe a lot of tax, it's wise to consider sending your return by certified mail, return receipt requested. Just remember that the receipt doesn't prove anything about what was inside the envelope you mailed—just that you mailed it on time and the IRS received it.

Computer and Telephone Filing

The IRS is committed to an electronic, paperless future.

More than 13.5 million taxpayers filed their returns electronically in 1994—and the IRS hopes to quadruple that number by the year 2000. By then, most of the rest may file on the phone.

Electronic filing for a fee began in 1986. Thousands of tax-return preparers provide this service via their computers, transmitting your tax information directly to computers at the IRS. Banks and IRS-approved businesses can also be hired to transmit your return this way.

Filing taxes by computer offers taxpayers several advantages over filing on paper. First, the IRS confirms electronically that it has received your return. That's surer for you than trusting the mail. Second, electronic filing eliminates data-entry errors at the IRS.

Filing electronically also means you'll get your refund faster. The IRS promises to issue refunds for electronic filers within three weeks. It will do it even faster if you choose to have the money deposited directly in your bank account by electronic transfer.

"INSTANT REFUNDS" CAN BE COSTLY

Many electronic-filing services offer to arrange an "instant refund" within a few days. What you really get is a **refund-anticipation loan**, with your refund as collateral.

Remember that an instant refund is a loan that uses your IRS refund as security

The lender charges you a fixed fee and requires you to tell the IRS to deposit your actual refund in your bank account. Then the lender collects the debt and the fee out of your account.

You get less money than you would if you waited a little longer for the full refund. Moreover, the loan fee usually works out to be a very high percentage if viewed as an annual interest rate.

The system has attracted many fraudulent refund claims, so the IRS has tightened the eligibility terms for electronic filing.

If you owe tax, you can file your electronic return as early as you like and wait until April 15 to send in a check.

Many states are teaming up with the IRS to offer combined electronic filing for federal and state returns.

ELECTRONIC PAPERWORK

Even electronic filers have to deal with a little paperwork. Your tax preparer will have you sign Form 8453, "U.S. Individual Income Tax Declaration for Electronic Filing," and will send it to the IRS for you. Make sure the agent gives you paper copies of this form, and your return, for your records.

If you file electronically and owe tax, your service should give you Form 9282 to mail with your check.

In 1994, the IRS received some 4.2 million 1040PC returns and 519,000 Telefile returns.

FILING ELECTRONICALLY
- Less paperwork
- File early—pay on April 15
- Reduces errors
- Faster refund
- IRS confirms electronically

USING A HOME COMPUTER
- Software available for tax record-keeping
- Print out 1040 PC to mail to IRS
- IRS can process 1040PCs faster and more accurately

FILING BY TELEPHONE
- Toll-free
- For 1040EZ filers who are invited by IRS
- 24-hour access
- Instant tax computation
- Need a push-button phone

FILING WITH YOUR OWN COMPUTER

Largely because of legal complications, using your home computer to file by linking electronically with the IRS is several years away. Off-the-shelf tax software, however, is a major step in this direction.

Most commercial programs compute your taxes and print out a condensed 1040 called Form 1040PC. The software can shrink an eleven-page 1040 to two pages of line numbers and dollar amounts on a 1040PC that you mail to the IRS.

Besides the luxury of storing your tax records on your hard disk, computerizing your taxes will speed up your refund. The IRS can process a paper 1040PC faster and more accurately than it can the full 1040.

FILING BY PHONE

If your taxes are simple enough to be figured on a 1040EZ, you may be able to file your return by push-button telephone. TeleFile is a 24-hour, toll-free service that allows taxpayers in a growing number of states to file this way. The option is available only to people who receive invitations in the mail from the IRS.

1040-TEL is a very quick way to file. The IRS computer will figure your adjusted gross income on the spot, and then tell you either the amount of your tax due or how much your refund will be. The call takes about five minutes. Afterward, the taxpayer signs and mails Form 1040-TEL to the IRS with a W-2 and a check, if there is a balance due.

Types of Audits

The IRS calls them examinations; taxpayers call them audits. Whatever you call them, they're not the end of the world.

The tax code requires you—not the IRS—to show that all the information on your tax return is correct. That is what audits are all about. Audits are designed to verify that you reported all your income and that you're entitled to all the dependency exemptions, deductions and credits you've claimed.

Everyone dreads IRS audits, although relatively few taxpayers face them. If you've done your best to file an accurate return and have good records, you probably shouldn't fret about an audit.

In the worst case, the auditor will find errors or you won't be able to back up a claim. If that happens, you'll get a bill for added taxes and interest. If the auditor thinks you've bent the law, you may be hit with a civil cash penalty for negligence or fraud. But keep in mind that auditors aren't authorized to investigate outright criminal tax evasion, and they rarely turn a case over to a tax-crime investigator.

You can appeal an audit finding to higher authorities within the IRS and to the federal courts. But you must be sure not to miss the deadlines set by the IRS for each step in the audit process.

THE OFFICE AUDIT

The **office audit** is conducted at an IRS district or regional office near you. These audits are the most common, accounting for nearly 48 percent of all personal audits in 1993. That year, 14 percent of office audits resulted in no change in taxes. The rest led to tax bills averaging $2,625.

THE CORRESPONDENCE AUDIT

The **correspondence audit** is done by mail. The IRS asks you to document a few items you reported on your return—perhaps a gain on the sale of stock or a casualty-loss deduction. You respond by sending back explanations, along with copies of the requested documents, by certified mail.

In 1993, the IRS did nearly 29 percent of its audits by mail. In 18 percent of these audits, the tax wasn't changed. In the remainder, auditors claimed additional taxes, interest and penalties averaging $2,974 per return.

THE FIELD AUDIT

A **field audit** is held at your place of business, even if it's your home. The revenue agent has the right to come to your office to check such things as inventory, but cannot enter your home unless you use it for business.

Because a field audit is complicated, you should probably consult a tax professional. You can give power of attorney to a representative and move your records to her office. If you do, your representative may insist that the audit be held there.

More than 23 percent of personal audits in 1993 were done in the field, and revenue agents wrote out tax bills averaging $13,547. About 8 percent of the field audits produced no change in taxes.

THE DOCUMENT-MATCHING PROGRAM

All the pieces of information the IRS receives have to fit together.

If they don't, it could be an innocent mistake or it could be something more serious.

1099 W-2 1040

Before the IRS chooses any returns for full-blown audits, its computers take a crack at all the returns. The software compares your entries with reports of your income and deductions from organizations such as banks, brokerage houses and mutual-fund companies. This procedure is called **document matching**. The documents the program checks include the W-2 form you received from your employer and all 1099s you received from financial institutions that paid you interest or dividends.

If an item on your tax return differs from a report, and a review of your return doesn't clear up the discrepancy, the IRS will send you a notice called a CP-2000. The notice may bill you for more tax and interest, and may even impose a penalty. But it will also give you a chance to explain the discrepancy and support your tax return.

immediately to ask for an explanation. Then ask what documents the IRS needs in order to clear up the matter.

The IRS is beginning to accept more explanations over the phone. But even so, always put your final response in writing. Give your name, address, Social Security number, phone number and any reference number that the IRS uses. Include copies of the IRS notice and any records—such as canceled checks—that support your claim. Do not send original documents.

CP-2000

Document matching isn't strictly an audit, but increasingly, it substitutes for one.

	Total in 1993	Taxes, interest and penalties sought
CP-2000s	4,300,000	$3.7 billion
Audits	1,059,000	$5.7 billion

The IRS is frequently criticized for doing too few audits to deter taxpayers from cheating. Officials point to document matching and scientific selection of returns for audits as reasons the IRS doesn't need to do more.

RESPONDING TO A CP-2000

The error shown on the CP-2000 notice could be yours, but it could also be an error by the organization providing the information, or by the IRS. Double-check every bit of information in the notice. Follow the instructions and reply promptly.

If you need more time to respond, write to the IRS and say so. You may need time to find a record, for example. If you don't understand the notice, write or telephone

Explain the alleged error that caused the notice, and why you believe your numbers are correct. Send your letter by certified mail and request a return receipt. Keep a file with copies of everything. These rules of thumb apply to all dealings with the IRS—not just CP-2000s.

Don't be surprised if you get more notices. But don't ignore them, either. The IRS has a reputation for sending confusing notices and for not keeping track of taxpayers' replies. If this happens to you, write or call the IRS at once for an explanation. Tell them you have already answered the first notice, and send a copy of your original letter.

What Triggers an Audit?

High income, or hints of hidden income and inflated deductions, increase your chances of setting off an audit.

By choosing you for an audit, the IRS isn't accusing you of cheating—although it may later. The audit indicates there are items on your return that have generated errors or require proof or an explanation. The IRS tries to select returns that are most likely to contain errors, omissions of income or padded deductions.

Most audits result from a computer formula based on auditing experience. The formula, called **DIF**—for **Discriminate Function System**—analyzes the entries on your return. IRS computers score returns for potential errors and false entries. The DIF standards are secret. The IRS says that only a handful of people know them.

High-scoring returns then go to human classifiers who screen them and choose those most likely to be "productive," that is, those that provide the best chance for collecting additional taxes, interest and penalties. (The IRS is working on an advanced computer-logic system that may replace this human review.) These returns are sent out to IRS district auditors, who then get in touch with you.

RED FLAGS

Besides high income, the IRS looks for "red flags" that increase your chances of being audited. Red flags are unusual or suspicious entries on your tax return that may cause the IRS to take a closer look.

The IRS also looks for clues of unreported income. For

example, there may be third-party reports of payments to you that don't appear on your return. The discrepancy may indicate that you have not declared all your income.

Another tip-off is an unusually low reported income for a usually lucrative occupation. Your mortgage interest and property taxes arouse suspicion if they

AUDIT TRIGGERS

- Unusual or suspicious entries
- Evidence of unreported income
- Low reported income for normally high-paying work
- Large deductions out of line with income
- Extensive business deductions
- Amended returns claiming refunds
- Deductions for bad debt
- Large depreciation and maintenance deductions for rental property
- Alimony paid or received
- Foreign investments
- Tax shelters

AUDIT DETONATOR

DANGER

suggest an opulent lifestyle on an ordinary income.

Large deductions that are out of line with income are also eye-catchers. You may have improperly deducted your child's private-school tuition as a charitable gift, or improperly deducted hospital bills or casualty losses that were reimbursed by insurance.

OTHER CLUES

IRS agents look for the appearance of bloated business expenses for travel and entertainment, and for business deductions that could disguise personal expenses. Personal use of a company car falls in this category. Home offices invite scrutiny, as do sideline businesses that always lose money. The IRS may think these businesses are really run for write-offs, not profit. If that's the case, the IRS will nullify your deductions of losses.

The IRS also considers tax shelters, alimony payments, foreign investments, bad-debt deductions and amended returns claiming refunds. Alarm bells sound if a schedule required to support a deduction or credit is incomplete or missing. Large depreciation and maintenance deductions for a rental property may also attract attention.

THE DREADED RANDOM AUDIT

Every few years, the IRS chooses a random small cross section of returns for audit. This **Taxpayer Compliance Measurement Program,** or **TCMP,** produces the data that are used to develop standards for enforcement and audit selection. The audits are exhaustive and require proof for every entry, line by line. For the unlucky taxpayer who's chosen in this lottery, there's no way out.

The next round of TCMP audits is scheduled for 1995. The IRS plans to audit the 1994 returns of about 93,000 individuals. About 68,000 will have some business income, many from a sole proprietorship or a partnership. The other 25,000 returns will come from taxpayers without business income.

THE BEST WAY TO AVOID AN AUDIT

The best way to avoid an audit is to fill out your return correctly, with all the required schedules. If you think the IRS may question a large deduction or credit, attach an explanation to your return when you file it. Include copies (not originals) of the supporting documents for unusually large claims.

AUDITS IN 1914
You think the IRS is tough now? When 357,598 taxpayers filed the first modern income-tax returns in 1914, they had to sign them under oath before tax officials. And the Bureau of Internal Revenue audited every one.

TAX TATTLERS
As unnerving and even unethical as it may seem, tax tattlers are rewarded. The IRS pays for specific information that identifies tax evaders. In fiscal year 1993, it gave $5.3 million, a record amount, to 829 tipsters whose disclosures led to the collection of more than $172 million.

Informers, whose names are kept secret, shouldn't expect a bonanza. Since the late 1960s, the IRS says, it has received more than 177,000 tips. But it found just over 8 percent of them helpful enough to merit rewards. The payoffs for useful tips averaged $1,772.

The rewards, naturally, are taxable.

Who Gets Audited

Yes, it's true: The IRS does focus on specific occupations.

Although the IRS audited under 1 percent of all personal returns in 1993, it cast a wider net over high-income individuals— especially sole proprietors who report their business income and expenses on Schedule C. An IRS report in 1993 rated the compliance of sole proprietors below 80 percent, compared to overall taxpayer compliance of 93 percent.

The IRS also zeroes in on particular types of businesses. Most tax chiseling, according to the IRS, occurs in cash businesses and in transportation, retailing and agriculture. In the past, audits have targeted airline pilots with side-line-business losses, mail-order ministers claiming tax exemptions, door-to-door salespeople, waiters who report low tip income and catfish farmers.

The IRS is also bearing down on independent contractors and their employers. Many "contractors" are really employees and should have payroll taxes withheld by their employers.

Anchorage 1.11%

San Franscisco 1.63%

Los Angeles 1.43%

Percentage of returns audited in selected IRS districts

Audits By Income

Income	Percentage of Returns Audited
Under $25,000	0.71%
$25–50,000	0.58%
$50–100,000	0.88%
$100,000+	4.03%
Schedule C under $25,000	2.24%
Schedule C $25–100,000	2.41%
Schedule C $100,000+	3.91%

WHIPSAW AUDITS
Sometimes the IRS audits people who make conflicting claims about the same source of income or who claim conflicting deductions. Sam, for example, deducts alimony payments he made to his ex-wife Sally. Yet Sally doesn't report the payments as taxable income. Instead, she claims the payments were for child support, making them tax-free to her and non-deductible by Sam.

In this case, the IRS claims that both must pay more taxes. This "whipsaw" strategy is how the IRS protects itself until the matter is resolved by an agreement among the taxpayers or by a court.

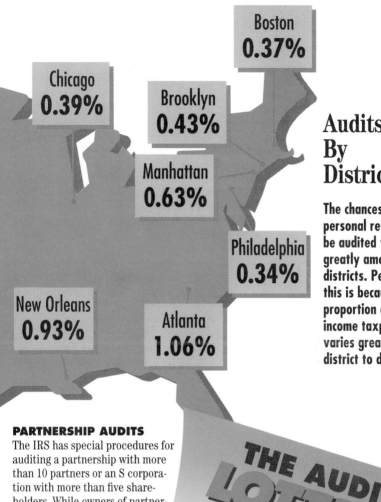

Boston
0.37%

Chicago
0.39%

Brooklyn
0.43%

Manhattan
0.63%

Philadelphia
0.34%

New Orleans
0.93%

Atlanta
1.06%

Audits By District

The chances that a personal return will be audited vary greatly among IRS districts. Perhaps this is because the proportion of high-income taxpayers varies greatly from district to district.

PARTNERSHIP AUDITS

The IRS has special procedures for auditing a partnership with more than 10 partners or an S corporation with more than five shareholders. While owners of partnerships and S corporations report the business's income and deductions on their personal returns, the IRS audits the firm before auditing the owners. The IRS generally notifies the owners that the firm is being audited. Owners of partnerships and S corporations may participate in the audit because it affects their personal returns.

THE AUDIT LOTTERY IRS

The proportion of personal tax returns that were audited has fallen over the years. Here's a look at the number of audits as a percentage of returns filed. The IRS's claims for added taxes, interest and penalties also are shown.

YEAR	NUMBER OF AUDITS	PERCENT OF RETURNS AUDITED	AMOUNT AUDITED
1963	3,495,000	0.49%	$839M
1973	1,409,000	1.75%	$1.1B
1983	1,428,000	1.50%	$3.9B
1993	1,059,000	0.92%	$5.7B

ESTATE-TAX AUDITS

Few Americans leave estates large enough to be taxed when they die. Only 70,000 estate-tax returns were filed in 1992. Of those, the IRS audited a healthy 17 percent.

The larger the estate, the greater the chance of an audit. In 1992, the IRS audited 53 percent of the returns for estates valued at more than $5 million.

Forewarned is Forearmed

Before you go into an audit, it's important to know your rights—as well as the IRS's.

It's your job—not the IRS's—to substantiate your claims. Like the entries on your return, the information you give in an audit is subject to the penalties of perjury. If an auditor believes you are deliberately being misleading, you may be slapped with a penalty.

If you don't show up for an audit or you refuse to supply records, the auditor can issue you a summons. The IRS can also issue a summons to third parties related to your case—banks, for example—to collect your records. This can have severe repercussions. If you ignore an IRS summons, the IRS can obtain a court order allowing it to send agents to "enforce the summons"—which means seizing any records, wherever they are. You can be arrested if you consistently ignore IRS summonses. If the IRS issues you a summons, you should see a lawyer.

TAXPAYERS' RIGHTS

By law, the IRS must tell you about your rights before the audit. It usually does this by sending you IRS Publication 1, "Your Rights as a Taxpayer." Read it carefully.

It tells you that taxpayers have the right to be treated fairly, courteously and promptly. You also have the right to speak to a supervisor if you think the auditor is not proceeding with the examination properly.

The auditor must start the meeting by explaining your rights and telling you what information the IRS wants and why. The auditor must also explain how the information will be used and what could happen if you don't cooperate.

The IRS must keep information about you private and confidential, except in certain circumstances. One important exception: Information from your audit may be sent to state tax authorities. For this reason, if an audit changes your federal tax, you should amend your state return as well.

THE IRS HAS DEADLINES, TOO

Normally, the IRS must audit your return and assess any added tax within three years after the return's due date, including filing extensions. However, the deadline is six years if you underreported your income by 25 percent or more. And there is no deadline at all if the return is fraudulent. A fraudulent return is one that is purposely intended to deceive the IRS about a significant tax issue.

The IRS usually sends notice of an audit 12 to 18 months after the return was filed. If you haven't received a notice within 18 months, the odds are that the return won't be audited.

EXTENDING THE STATUTE

The IRS's three-year period for assessing taxes against you is known as the **statute of limitation**. If the IRS sees its deadline approaching before it has finished your audit, the auditor will ask you to sign Form 872, "Consent to Extend the Time to Assess Tax." That's called "extending the statute."

If you don't sign, the auditor will send you a deficiency notice that decides all the issues in the IRS's favor and forces you to go to court to appeal your case.

Tax professionals advise you to sign a consent form unless you are eager to go to court. But they urge you not to accept an unlimited agreement that makes every item on your return an open issue for an indefinite term. Press instead for an extension that applies only to a few specific issues and that expires in three to six months. Of course, you may be asked to extend the statute again.

WHAT THE IRS CAN DO

- Demand to see your tax-related documents
- Ask about items not included in the audit notice
- Issue a summons if you miss your audit meeting
- Share your tax information with your state's tax authorities and foreign governments
- Ask you questions about other people
- Make an audio recording of the audit meeting
- Ask for an audit meeting at your home office
- Propose changes in your return and impose penalties and interest

WHAT YOU CAN DO

- Produce only the documents the IRS requests
- Ask for more time to find documents or stop the interview to consult a tax adviser
- Ask for your audit to be postponed or the site to be changed
- Ask for an explanation from your auditor or a supervisor
- Bring a representative, friend or witness
- Bring your taping equipment or buy the IRS's recording
- Not allow the IRS to inspect the non-business part of your home
- Appeal the audit findings to the IRS appeals office or a court

The IRS will change the date, the hour or the place of your audit if you have a good reason and give the auditor fair notice. You may have an important business trip that can't be rescheduled, for example, or you may need more time to find records.

You can also ask to change the site of the audit. Suppose you live in New Jersey but own a business in New York City and keep your records there. It probably will be more convenient for everyone if the audit is conducted by the IRS's Manhattan District rather than by the Newark District, which sent the notice originally. But the IRS has the last word on the time and the place of the meeting.

The IRS tries to avoid repetitious audits unless it suspects deliberately bad behavior. If you were audited within the past two years for the same items as those listed in the latest notice, and the auditor made no change in your taxes before, call the IRS. It may drop the audit, at least of those items.

IF THE IRS ASKS YOU ABOUT SOMEONE ELSE

You have no right to protect another person by withholding information from the IRS. But even if the IRS agent says you aren't a target of an investigation, be careful about answering questions that could connect you in some way to a crime. You always have the right to withhold information that could incriminate you.

If you're questioned about a business associate or an employer, for example, you may say something that leads the agent to suspect your involvement. To play it safe, you may tell the agent that you want to consult a lawyer before answering questions.

NOT TAKING THE FIFTH

The Fifth Amendment to the Constitution gives you the right not to incriminate yourself. But because audits aren't criminal investigations, you don't have the right to refuse to give the IRS information about your income and your tax return unless you will expose yourself to investigation for a crime. Remember, the IRS is only trying to substantiate something you signed.

If your responses during an audit might implicate you in any crime, stop the audit and retain a lawyer. Also consult a lawyer any time you plan on taking the Fifth.

The Audit Meeting

The best strategy is to be prompt, calm, reasonable and cooperative—and don't volunteer answers to questions that haven't been asked!

PREPARING FOR AN AUDIT

- Go over the audit notice to see that the information is correct and that you understand what the IRS wants.

- Review your return to see that you know how you arrived at every entry.

- Find and organize your records. You're more credible if you're well-organized and cooperative.

- Identify possible problems, such as missing documentation.

- Do some research on the tax laws applying to your audit. Read the instructions for the tax form and relevant IRS publications to get some hints as to why the IRS is questioning your return.

- Read "Your Rights as a Taxpayer," IRS Publication 1. It comes with the audit notice.

DO YOU NEED HELP?

You can probably handle an audit yourself if the stakes are small, and you have good records and nothing to hide. It doesn't make sense to pay a tax adviser $500 to save $200 in taxes—unless the peace of mind is worth the difference.

Your main risk in facing the audit alone is that you may say the wrong thing and suddenly find the auditor reaching for other items or even your tax returns from previous years.

Once the audit begins, you may realize you need professional help because it's going badly. The auditor must stop the interview if you want to consult a tax adviser or bring in a representative. If the auditor brings up tax fraud, stop the interview and consult a lawyer.

If you know from the outset that you have a complex issue that could lead to hefty taxes and penalties, you may hire a lawyer, a certified public accountant or an enrolled agent to speak for you at the audit. You may even stay home and send a representative in your place by giving her power of attorney on IRS Form 2848.

DURING THE AUDIT

WHAT TO EXPECT AT THE MEETING

The audit notice will tell you to bring canceled checks, receipts and other documentation. Bring it all, and be prepared to cover the topics on your audit notice. Leave unrelated records at home. That will help you to avoid volunteering information about your income, property and spending that the auditor doesn't ask for.

Auditors look for unreported income and phony business deductions, so be prepared to explain big bank-account deposits and checks. It's always a good idea to say you are sure you can prove your case if given more time.

It may be expensive, but a tax expert who is a shrewd bargainer may wrap up the matter faster than you can. Many IRS auditors prefer to deal with professionals who understand the issues and procedures and speak tax language.

An alternative is to ask your return preparer or a tax professional to advise you what to do yourself. That will save the fee for having the professional represent you. Get an analysis of the issues and the pros and cons of going it alone.

You may also take along your spouse, a relative, a friend or your business's bookkeeper for moral support or to help answer questions.

DON'T ADVERTISE
Be cautious in conversations with relatives and acquaintances, tax experts suggest. Try not to let employees and customers know you are being audited. A disgruntled colleague, employee or ex-spouse may volunteer to help the IRS audit you.

SOME OTHER TIPS

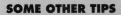

- Stick to the items in the notice.

- Ask the auditor who brings up topics not listed in the notice to send you another written notice to which you will respond later.

- Avoid playful remarks that might be taken as bribes. Offering favors can get you into trouble.

- Keep track of every item on which you disagree with the auditor, and review the list with the auditor at the end of the interview.

- Ask to speak to the auditor's supervisor if you need further explanation.

A TIP ON TAPING
You must give the IRS written notice 10 days in advance of the audit meeting if you want to make an audio recording of it. You must bring your own taping equipment. If the IRS wants to make a recording, it will give you 10 days' notice and offer to sell you a copy.

Many tax advisers are wary of recordings. Taping audit meetings is a relatively infrequent occurrence and can signal to the IRS an uncooperative attitude on your part.

WHAT'S NEXT? THE EXAMINATION REPORT

If your audit went smoothly, the auditor will hand you an **Examination Report,** Form 4549, at the end of the interview. More likely, the auditor will mail the report to you. It will list and explain any changes—what the IRS calls **adjustments**—that the auditor proposes to make to your return.

If you agree with the changes, sign Form 870, "Consent to Proposed Tax Adjustments," and return it with a check. Do this if the IRS's claims are correct, or if you feel like paying up to be done with the matter.

If you do nothing after getting the examination report, the auditor will turn in a report describing the points in dispute. Within a few weeks, you'll get a 30-day letter.

THE 30-DAY AND 90-DAY LETTERS

The 30-day letter confirms that your case is "unagreed" and gives you 30 days to appeal to the IRS without going to court. The 30-day letter also tells you how to appeal to the IRS.

30 DAYS TO APPEAL

90 DAYS TO APPEAL

If you don't appeal or pay the tax bill within 30 days, the IRS will send you a **Statutory Notice of Deficiency,** also known as the 90-day letter. This deficiency notice is the jumping-off point for going to court. If you want to contest the IRS's claims in the **U.S. Tax Court**, you must petition the court within 90 days after the date of the notice.

That's an important deadline. The Tax Court is your last resort for an appeal without first paying the IRS's bill in full. If you miss that deadline and still want to fight the IRS, you must pay the bill and sue for a refund in one of the other federal courts.

Appealing an Audit

If you believe you're right and the auditor is wrong, you can appeal. But know the rules before you play the game.

The IRS offers its own appeals process for contesting the results of an audit. Naturally, this is the route favored by the IRS, and many tax experts suggest you follow it. You often save time and expense, and the chances are fairly good that an **appeals officer** will settle for less than the auditor would.

Appeals officers come from a regional department that's separate from the district office that audited you. Their goal is to settle cases. Unlike auditors, they consider the possible costs to the IRS of letting you go to court. The auditor does not take part in your appeal.

FILING YOUR APPEAL

You must write to your district director to request an appeal. Your request will be forwarded to the appeals office.

You don't have to include a written statement outlining your appeal if you had an office or a correspondence audit. Nor is a written protest necessary if the amount in question in a field audit is under $2,500. However, tax experts advise you to attach at least a brief statement of the IRS claims that your are disputing and why you disagree with them.

FRIVOLOUS CLAIMS

Judges penalize people who bring suits to delay paying taxes or who make frivolous tax protests. The Tax Court can impose a penalty of up to $25,000 in these cases. One Florida man was convicted of failing to file tax returns for six years, yet he told the Tax Court he didn't owe taxes because he headed the Church of the Everlasting Return. The court told him to pay $80,000 in taxes and civil fraud penalties, plus $5,000 for wasting its time with frivolous claims.

MAKING YOUR CASE

It's a good idea to consult a tax professional before filing an appeal and going to the appeals conference. You should decide in advance what you are willing to give up to

IF YOU **DISAGREE** WITH THE AUDITORS

YOU CAN APPEAL TO THE IRS

AT ANY POINT IN THE PROCESS

- You can agree and arrange to pay the tax
- You can ask for a notice of deficiency so you can file a petition with the Tax Court
- You can pay the tax and file a claim for a refund

settle the case, and you should develop a bargaining strategy.

You can take a representative with you to the appeals conference or send one in your place. You can also bring witnesses to support your case.

Your job is to show the appeals officer that you have strong factual support for your position and that you have a chance of winning at least a partial victory in court. Take plenty of time to prepare your records and rehearse your presentation.

If your appeals conference ends without a settlement, you'll soon be mailed a 90-day deficiency notice. Then you must decide whether to pay or go to the Tax Court.

PETITIONING THE TAX COURT

The Tax Court tries only civil cases brought by taxpayers to contest federal deficiency notices. It doesn't handle criminal cases, which are prosecuted by the government in U.S. district courts.

The IRS deficiency notice will tell you how to petition the Tax Court to review your case. It's vital to have your petition postmarked by a U.S. post office within 90 days after the date the notice was mailed, not the date you

THE TAX COURT ODDS

The odds favor the IRS. But by the IRS's own reckoning, taxpayers come away with something in more than half of the Tax Court cases that are tried and decided. In fiscal 1993, the IRS says, it won 688 decisions, lost 122, and split 612. In a split ruling, the judge rules for the IRS on some issues and for the taxpayer on others.

IF YOU STILL DISAGREE AND DON'T PAY

YOU CAN APPEAL TO THE TAX COURT

Only regular Tax Court decisions may be appealed to higher courts.

You can request a deficiency notice from the IRS so you can file a petition to the Tax Court.

IF YOU STILL DISAGREE AND PAY

YOU CAN SUE FOR A REFUND

You can appeal a refund claim all the way to the Supreme Court.

You can file suit to reclaim your money in federal claims or district court.

received it. (The period is 150 days if the notice was mailed to you outside the U.S.)

You may be represented in the Tax Court by anyone admitted by that court to practice there. If you have a lot at stake, you will probably need an experienced tax counsel. If the amount at issue is under $10,000, you may ask the court to handle your case using the more informal small-case procedures.

There are no jury trials in the Tax Court. Decisions in small cases may not be appealed to higher federal courts. However, decisions in regular cases may be appealed to U.S. appeals courts and all the way to the Supreme Court.

One advantage of going to the Tax Court is that you may represent yourself. Many taxpayers do this. But although the court will instruct you in its procedures, it's wise to consult a tax professional.

Tax Court judges try to get cases settled before trial. Most cases are. If you didn't use the IRS appeals process before petitioning the court, the judge will ask you to meet with an IRS appeals officer.

COURTS OF LAST RESORT

Most taxpayers choose to go to the Tax Court because they don't have to pay IRS claims before getting a hearing. Other U.S. trial courts hear taxpayer suits for refunds of taxes already paid. At the end of fiscal 1993, there were 41,900 cases pending in the Tax Court and 2,100 refund cases pending in other U.S. trial courts.

If you miss the Tax Court's petition deadline or choose not to petition the court, your last recourse is to pay your tax bill and sue for a refund.

You may file a refund suit in the U.S. Claims Court in Washington, D.C. Like the Tax Court, the U.S. Claims Court doesn't hold jury trials. If you want a jury trial, or a judge who isn't a tax-law specialist, you may sue for a refund in your Federal District Court.

There are rules and time limits for suing for a refund. IRS Publication 556, "Examination of Returns, Appeal Rights and Claims for Refund," will provide more information.

You'll probably need a lawyer to represent you in one of these courts, although you may represent yourself. The IRS is represented by its own lawyers in the Tax Court and by Justice Department lawyers in other courts.

THE TAX COURT: HOW IT WORKS

The Tax Court began in 1924 as the Board of Tax Appeals. It became a court in 1942. There are 19 Tax Court judges, all appointed by the president. There are also special judges who hear small cases where the amount at issue is no more than $10,000 for any year.

The Tax Court is based at 400 Second Street, N.W., Washington, D.C. 20217. But its judges travel around the country for trials and pre-trial hearings. Your Tax Court case would be heard in the federal court building near you.

Negotiating a Better Deal

The IRS's demand for payment is not necessarily the end of the road. Often, you can still make a deal.

If you don't pay all the tax you owe, you'll get a **Notice of Tax Due and Demand for Payment.** This notice starts the collection process. You will get one if you don't pay all the tax due with your return or if you owe tax after you've been audited and have exhausted your appeals.

Even if you are able and willing to pay the tax and the interest and penalties on the bill, check the amounts. If you think an amount is incorrect, ask for a correction by calling, writing or visiting the IRS. As always, when you have a dispute with the IRS, be prepared to provide copies of canceled checks, receipts or other documents showing payments or arrangements to pay. Keep a complete file of all your correspondence.

The notice will tell you how to contact the IRS, or you can call 1-800-829-1040. When you call, ask for Publication 594, "Understanding the Collection Process," and Publication 1, "Your Rights as a Taxpayer."

> ## PAY YOUR BACK TAXES, INTEREST AND PENALTIES IN FULL, NOW!

ACTS OF GOD

Even though you concede you owe the tax, you may ask to have penalties (but not interest) canceled for "reasonable cause." The IRS calls this **abatement.**

Your serious illness or the death or illness of someone in your family may be reasonable cause for your filing a return late or making a late payment. Other reasonable causes include the loss of your records by fire or flood, reliance on a tax preparer who gave you bad advice, or the failure of an employer or bank to give you information in time.

You can even win an abatement if you show you relied on wrong advice you received from the IRS in writing or over the phone.

Of course, you'll need hard evidence of the reasonable cause. You'll need to show that you couldn't comply with the law even though you used "ordinary business care and prudence."

You can request an abatement by writing to the IRS Service Center that sent you your tax bill. If your request is denied, you can appeal by requesting a reconsideration.

The IRS says it abated nearly 128,000 personal penalties for reasonable cause in 1993, giving up claims for $73 million.

Billpayer's Rights

You still have rights even though you lost your audit appeal and owe money. Here are some of your rights as a billpayer:

- You may consult a tax professional or turn the matter over to one.

- You may ask to pay in installments.

- If you can prove that paying would cause a hardship for you, you may ask to delay the start of payments.

- The IRS's **Problem Resolution Office** can help you if a collection demand is causing such a hardship that you can't pay for food, housing or medical care.

- You can make an offer in compromise, asking the IRS to settle for less than what you owe.

- You are entitled to a copy of any payment agreement that you make and to receipts for payments.

- If you go into bankruptcy proceedings, the IRS will stop enforcement actions temporarily. You will need the advice of a lawyer in this situation.

But gosh, it wasn't <u>my</u> fault!

But I can't pay it <u>all</u> at once!

YIKES! That's more than I'll <u>ever</u> have!

LET'S MAKE A DEAL

If you're sure you will never be able to pay all you owe, this is the deal for you. The IRS may allow you to clean your slate for a few cents on the dollar. The key is being able to prove your case to the IRS.

You can make an **offer in compromise** on IRS Form 656. You'll have to submit a financial statement and offer to pay the most that you think you can afford. The IRS may ask for more, including a share of your future earnings. But it does have the power to settle for less than the full amount you owe in tax, interest and penalties.

The IRS has the last word on any deal. Once you reach an agreement with the IRS, stick to it. If you can't, tell the IRS and try to work out a new agreement that you can live up to.

BUDGET BUSTERS

Your best strategy is to respond promptly to an IRS tax bill and, if it's correct, to pay as much as you can by the deadline. If you can't pay it all, tell the IRS right away that you need an installment plan, a delay in payment or a compromise settlement. Remember that interest charges keep piling up as long as you owe the IRS anything.

The IRS may ask for details on your financial condition. In recent years, the IRS has been more generous in agreeing to installment payments and compromise settlements. You may have to sell assets or borrow money to pay taxes, though. And the IRS will keep any refund you have coming for past years.

A DEAL WITH A TWANG

Willie Nelson, the country-music singer, composed a big compromise settlement with the IRS. After some unwise tax-shelter investments collapsed, Nelson owed the IRS $16.7 million in taxes, interest and penalties that he couldn't pay. The IRS seized and auctioned off many of his possessions and took a big cut of his recording income. But the IRS wound up with only $3.6 million, far less than Nelson owed.

Then Nelson's tax advisers proposed an offer in compromise that the IRS accepted. Nelson agreed to pay a total of $9 million by the end of five years. If he keeps the bargain, he escapes further IRS claims on his assets and income.

Criminal Investigations

Major tax crimes include evasion, fraud, failure to file, filing a false return and aiding the filing of a false return.

CRIMINAL

Prosecutions are court actions meant to punish intentional violations of the law.

They may lead to:
- Fines
- Imprisonment

CIVIL

Audits are administrative reviews that verify the entries on taxpayers' returns.

They may lead to:
- Penalties and interest
- Liens and levies
- Seizure of property

Tax crimes are worse than violations of civil law. They can result in crippling fines and imprisonment. The best known tax crime, **tax evasion**, is the willful or intentional attempt to evade taxes or to break the tax laws in any way. The maximum penalty for an individual is a $250,000 fine and five years in prison.

Filing an intentionally false or fraudulent return can be punished by a fine of up to $100,000 and a prison term of up to three years. Intentional failure to file a return is punishable by a fine of up to $25,000 and a prison term of up to one year for each missing return. It's also a crime to advise or assist someone in the intentional filing of a false or fraudulent return.

OTHER CRIMES INCLUDE THE FAILURE TO:

- **Pay tax owed**
- **Keep proper records**
- **Supply tax information**
- **Obey a summons by the IRS**

The government must start its prosecution within six years after the commission of a major tax crime. In every case, the prosecutors must prove beyond a reasonable doubt that the violation was intentional.

The IRS doesn't stop its efforts when a criminal case is ended by a conviction or an acquittal. Either way, the IRS will go after the tax allegedly due and will probably impose heavy civil penalties for negligence or fraud.

IRS INVESTIGATIONS

IRS auditors who uncover evidence of unreported income refer cases of possible tax crimes to the IRS's criminal-investigation division (CID). The CID also gets leads from law-enforcement agencies such as the Federal Bureau of Investigation, the Drug Enforcement Agency and local police.

The CID stages "sting" operations with undercover agents to trap suspected tax cheats. An agent may pose as the prospective buyer of a business and catch the owner bragging that the business hides a good deal of unreported cash income.

People with grudges—often ex-spouses or ex-employees—slip tips to the CID. In their investigations, special agents speak to a suspect's business associates, advisers, fellow employees, friends, neighbors,

THE GOOD-FAITH DEFENSE
If you believed, in "good faith," that you weren't violating the law by not paying taxes, you lacked criminal intent and can't be convicted of a tax crime. So says the Supreme Court. But that doesn't excuse you from paying taxes.

bankers, tax preparers and accountants.

But the IRS can't force a lawyer to talk about a client's affairs. Federal law protects the confidentiality of communications between lawyers and their clients. However, there's no such protection for communications between accountants, including certified public accountants, and their clients.

IF YOU'RE A TARGET

The IRS isn't likely to tell you that you're being investigated for a possible tax crime until an agent is well prepared to interrogate you. But someone who has already been interviewed by the IRS may tell you of an investigation about you. Or you may notice that an IRS auditor who was once eager to get more information or records from you has suddenly stopped pressing you for them. That happens because the IRS must suspend its civil investigation of you when possible criminal issues arise.

If you have any reason to suspect that you are the target of a criminal investigation, you should retain a lawyer who is experienced in criminal tax matters. The lawyer will advise you not to say anything to anybody about your business or tax affairs.

A special agent who speaks to you must tell you whether you are under criminal investigation. If you are, the agent must inform you of your rights to remain silent and to be represented by a lawyer. Exercise those rights immediately. Don't answer questions and don't volunteer information or make comments. Get a lawyer.

THE AUDIT TRAIL DOESN'T ALWAYS LEAD TO COURT

The IRS finds plenty of tax cheats through audits. Most are slapped with negligence and civil fraud penalties. Yet the IRS chooses to accuse very few of these people of criminal actions. Prosecution requires going to court, and takes a lot of proof, time and money. The IRS doesn't have to go to court to impose a civil fraud penalty.

"We don't pay taxes. Only the little people pay taxes."

PERPETRATOR: Tex E. Vader
CHARGES: Failure To File

PROSECUTING TAX CHEATS

If the government decides to make a public example of a tax cheat, it's almost sure to win a conviction. Just ask Leona Helmsley, the former queen of New York hoteliers, who was heard by her housekeeper to say: "We don't pay taxes. Only the little people pay taxes." The housekeeper's testimony about that indiscreet remark helped to send Mrs. Helmsley to prison for willful tax evasion.

When the IRS refers a case to criminal prosecutors in the U.S. Department of Justice, it isn't trying to collect unpaid taxes. The IRS can go after the money on its own. While tax prosecutions punish an outrageous crime, they are also designed to get as much publicity as possible for the conviction. Publicity may make a lot of other people back away from cheating on their taxes.

Although tax prosecutions are rare, the rate of convictions is high. The IRS and the U.S. district attorneys who are part of the Justice Department don't decide to bring charges unless they are confident of winning. In 1993, when 114.2 million personal returns were filed, the IRS began only 3,281 investigations of tax crimes not connected with narcotics or other crimes. These and previous investigations led to 1,643 indictments and 1,550 convictions. Of the 1,458 convicted tax criminals who were sentenced during that year, 60 percent went to prison.

THE IRS OFFERS LENIENCY TO MANY NON-FILERS

The IRS estimates that up to 10 million Americans a year who should file income-tax returns don't. It believes that many of these people don't file because of ignorance, confusion, inability to pay, personal problems or fear—and not because they are crooks at heart.

As a result, the IRS has offered lenient treatment to non-filers who join the tax system voluntarily. It promises to waive criminal prosecution of those who come forward to file delinquent returns before being approached by IRS crime investigators. It also invites non-filers to propose installment-payment plans or compromise settlements.

This isn't a true amnesty that eliminates all penalties. But it's as close to amnesty as anything the IRS is likely to offer.

MISSING PERSONS

There Is a Season

Tax planning never stops. And it makes sense for everyone—not just the wealthy.

No one can take a job, buy a house, get married, raise children, invest money or start a business without plunging into a sea of tax implications. While those implications are daunting, there are helpful principles you can use to keep your head well above water.

GETTING STARTED: TAKE STOCK OF WHAT YOU HAVE

The best way to start tax planning is to analyze what you have now. That list includes your job, your home, your family, your life- and health-insurance plans and your retirement program. Most people start with their latest tax return and run scenarios. What can you do to ease the tax bite next time around? What about your deductions and credits? How can you keep better records of your deductible expenses?

Fourth Quarter

Now is the time to estimate what your tax bill is going to be for the entire year and make year-end financial decisions to lessen that bill. If you don't expect your tax rate to rise in the coming year, you may want to delay part of your tax payment for a year by shifting some of your income into January. You may want to pay off deductible expenses in December to lower this year's tax. See page 104 for more on year-end tax maneuvers.

If you know you are going to earn a lot of capital gains for the year, consider selling stock at a loss to offset the gains before December 31.

If you are planning to set up a tax-deferred Keogh plan, you must do it by December 31. You don't have to put any money into the Keogh plan until your return is due—usually April 15 of the following year. If you get an extension, you can wait even longer.

If your employer offers a salary-reduction plan in which you take some of your pay as tax-free fringe benefits (see p. 97), you'll be asked to enroll during the fourth quarter for the following year.

First Quarter

The months up to April 15 are known as the tax season. The season's first deadline is on January 15, when you must pay the final estimated-tax bill for the previous year, if you owe the tax.

By the end of January, you should receive a W-2 wage statement from your employer and Form 1099s and similar tax-related statements from your bank, your stockbrokerage firm and others. It's a good idea to assemble these records as they arrive, choose the proper tax form and do some preliminary

> **Anyone may so arrange his affairs that his taxes shall be as low as possible; he is not bound to choose the pattern which will best pay the Treasury; there is not even a patriotic duty to increase one's taxes.**
>
> —Appeals Court Judge Learned Hand, 1934

figuring to find out whether you can expect a refund. The sooner you file your return, the sooner you'll bank a refund.

If you aren't due for a refund, make sure you'll have enough money on hand on April 15 to pay your tax bill for the previous year. If you're subject to estimated taxes for the current year (see p. 46), you'll need cash on April 15 for the first payment, too.

You have until April 15 to make a contribution for the previous year to an IRA. Retirement-savings contributions to SEPs and Keogh plans for the previous year are due April 15, unless you get a return-filing extension.

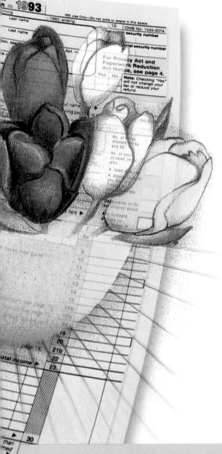

PRINCIPLES TO KEEP IN MIND

1 Don't think of tax planning as something you do only once a year when preparing to file your tax return. To be really effective, tax planning must continue throughout the year.

2 Professional advisers caution you to be wary of making financial decisions—especially investment decisions—for tax reasons alone. It's the total payoff that counts, not the immediate tax savings. Tax-free earnings from a municipal bond, or "muni," for example, may yield less over time than the after-tax gain from a taxable investment.

3 Develop a long-term financial and tax strategy, and make short-term moves to fit that strategy.

4 In shopping for investments, remember the difference between **tax-deferred** and **tax-free** (or **tax-exempt**) income. If the income is tax-free, such as the interest from a municipal bond, you'll never have to pay federal tax on it. If the income is tax-deferred, such as retirement-plan earnings or the increase in a stock's value while you hold the stock, you delay paying taxes until you withdraw the plan earnings or sell the stock.

Second and Third Quarters

In the wake of tax season, the second quarter is the time to evaluate your long-term strategy. Review your return and make mid-term corrections.

If your tax bill for last year was higher than it needed to be, see whether tax-exempt or tax-deferred investments would trim the bill for this year and fit into your long-term strategy. If you received a big refund for last year, you may want to have less money withheld from your paycheck or refigure estimated-tax payments for this year. If you had to pay a lot on April 15, consider having more tax withheld or upping your estimated-tax payments.

If you received a return-filing extension in April, your return is due on August 15. But the dates of your estimated-tax payments don't change.

Planning On the Job

The way you handle your pay, benefits and retirement plans has a big effect on your tax bill.

The largest share of most people's taxable income is what they earn on the job. A good way to begin planning for your taxes is to look for 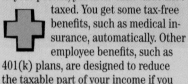 ways to cut the taxable part of your earnings and to take advantage of benefits that give you a tax break for certain expenses, such as medical bills.

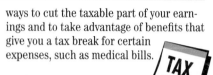

TAX-FREE BENEFITS

 Many employee benefits are like money in your pocket, yet their cash value isn't taxed. You get some tax-free benefits, such as medical insurance, automatically. Other employee benefits, such as 401(k) plans, are designed to reduce the taxable part of your income if you put your own money into them. Take time to learn what's available to you.

The law permits employers to give tax-free subsidies to employees for the cost of getting to work. It's up to the employer to do this. The limit is $60 a month for bus or train fare or for the cost of sharing a van that seats at least seven people. An employer may subsidize up to $155 a month of an employee's cost of parking at the job—tax-free.

Through 1994, the law permitted an employer to give up to $5,250 a year—tax-free—to an employee to pay for education, whether or not it was related to the job. Congress is likely to renew this benefit, so watch for it.

TAXABLE BENEFITS

 Many employee benefits are taxable, including the personal use of a company car, a personal trip on the company plane, a country-club membership and group term life insurance that exceeds $50,000. Generally, your employer figures the value of the benefits under IRS rules and adds it to the pay shown on your W-2. But your employer may choose not to withhold taxes on your non-cash income, so you may have to pay more tax on April 15 than you expected. Keep track of the value of the income, and be prepared to come up with the tax money. You may even have to pay estimated taxes on these benefits, if they increase your earnings substantially.

DEFERRED COMPENSATION

Many companies offer special plans to executives who can afford to wait for some of their money until they retire or leave the company. To take advantage of these plans, you may elect in a written agreement to defer part of your salary or your bonus before you earn it.

You aren't taxed on this income, or on any interest it may accumulate, until you receive it years later, presumably when your tax rate will be lower. However, under certain circumstances, the money taken out at a later date may be subject to Social Security taxes. Before making such an agreement, you may want to consult an adviser. One caveat: Since the deferred compensation is not protected by pension-fund regulations, you may want to make sure that the company will have the money to pay you when the time comes.

A HIDDEN BENEFIT

Flexible-spending and deferred-compensation plans offer an advantage that you may not notice. They reduce adjusted gross income, or AGI, which is the basis for many limits on personal exemptions and itemized deductions.

If you are in a high-income bracket and subject to broad limits on personal exemptions and itemized deductions, you may minimize or escape the effects of the limits by lowering your AGI. You may also slip past the specific limits on certain deductions, such as medical expenses and IRA contributions.

FLEXIBLE-SPENDING PLANS

A flexible-spending plan gives you the option of taking part of your pay as tax-free fringe benefits. The choices may include health insurance, payment of medical costs that aren't covered by insurance, life insurance and dependent care. The arrangements, sometimes called **cafeteria** or **salary-reduction plans**, are valuable because they let you cut your taxable income without losing the use of the money.

If you contribute money to one of these plans, it gets taken out of your paycheck and put into an account for you. You aren't taxed on the money you set aside. As you run up bills for those benefits, the company either pays them or reimburses you out of your account.

Here's how it works: Suppose you set aside $1,000 for medical bills that aren't paid in full by insurance. You aren't taxed on the $1,000. If your federal tax rate is 28 percent, you've saved $280 to pay medical bills (more, if you take state and local income taxes into account). That's cash you probably couldn't save by taking the $1,000 as an itemized deduction, because of the severe limit on medical deductions.

A flexible-spending plan is a great way to cut taxes, but going into one takes some study. You must decide before a year starts how much to set aside during that year. You'll need to review previous expenses to come up with a good estimate. Once your decision takes effect, you can't alter it unless there's a change in your family status.

Remember: If you don't use all the money in a flexible-spending account by year's end, you lose it.

There's a major drawback to a flexible-spending plan: If you don't spend all the money in your account by year's end, you lose all of the unused amount. It isn't refunded to you or carried over to the next year.

There's another potential drawback to putting money into a flexible-spending plan for the care of children or other dependents. Reimbursements received under the plan will reduce the amount of spending that qualifies for the dependent-care credit. You'll have to figure the value of the credit to decide whether it or the flexible-spending plan is a better choice for you.

How Flexible-Spending Plans Work

Money you set aside in a flexible-spending plan to pay for your medical bills that are not covered by insurance is not taxed. Here's what someone in the 28 percent tax bracket would save if she paid her medical expenses through a flexible-spending plan.

LOSE $280 TO TAXES

OR

SAVE $280 ON TAXES

WITHOUT FLEXIBLE SPENDING

	$1,000	Income paid for non-deductible medical expenses
−	280	Tax
=	$ 720	HOW MUCH YOU HAVE LEFT TO SPEND

WITH FLEXIBLE SPENDING

	$1,000	Income set aside in a flexible-spending plan
−	0	Tax
=	$1,000	HOW MUCH YOU HAVE TO SPEND

Because it's hard to estimate exactly how much money you'll spend through a flexible-spending plan, tax experts advise you to set aside less money than you expect you'll need. Still, if you can predict big medical expenses that you know aren't covered and if you can control their timing, as with dental work, you may be able to cram them all into one year. Then you can set aside the maximum flexible-spending amount with the confidence that nothing will be left unspent, and lost, at the end of the year.

STOCK OPTIONS

Incentive stock options, or ISOs, let executives buy their company's stock at a discount and get a tax break when they sell it. An ISO generally won't trigger tax until the executive sells the stock bought by **exercising** the option. Then the tax generally is figured at the favorable capital-gains rate (28 percent in 1994). However, exercising an ISO may trigger the alternative minimum tax. See IRS Publication 550, "Investment Income and Expenses."

Tax-Deferred Savings

Some of the best tax-planning bets are company retirement-savings plans, or those you set up on your own.

Tax-deferred savings plans let you invest money so that earnings accumulate without being taxed until you begin to make withdrawals. Retirement plans that qualify for tax deferral generally keep you from using the money until you retire or leave your job. Even then you are taxed only on what you take out.

Another advantage of pension plans, 401(k) plans, individual retirement accounts and Keogh plans is that when you withdraw the money, your tax rate is likely to be lower than the rate you pay when you are working and have more income. See IRS Publication 554, "Tax Information for Older Americans."

COMPANY RETIREMENT PLANS

The usual pension and profit-sharing plans are funded mainly by employers. You may be allowed to add some of your pay to them, but it may be "after-tax" money. That means you have already paid income tax on it. But you still have the advantage of deferring taxes on the earnings in your account. And you won't have to pay tax on after-tax contributions when you withdraw them.

401(K) PLANS

Named for a tax-code section, 401(k) plans have become an increasingly popular alternative to the usual company retirement plans. 401(k)s offer the same benefits as salary-reduction plans: You reduce your pay by having money withheld and deposited in a tax-deferred retirement-savings plan. You don't pay income tax on your contribution in the year you make it, although you do pay Social Security tax on it.

Company plans usually set contribution limits based on your salary. The law sets an annual maximum on your contribution that's indexed for inflation. In 1994, the maximum 401(k) contribution was $9,235. Many employers help by making matching contributions. Usually these are fixed at a certain percentage of the amount you are putting away.

How Tax Deferral Works

With a taxable investment, you have to pay taxes on the earnings each year. If that amount were invested in a tax-deferred account, the after-tax bite at the time of withdrawal would be less.

Here is a comparison of two $10,000 after-tax investments over 30 years, compounded monthly. One is tax-deferred, the other isn't. The example assumes you are single and in the 36 percent bracket.

WITH A TAXABLE PLAN... **YOU PAY TAX ON ALL EARNINGS ANNUALLY**

for example

$	10,000	invested
+	16,289	30 years of earnings at 5%, taxed annually at 36 percent
=	$26,289	**WHAT'S LEFT AFTER TAXES**

I.O. ME

LENDING TO YOURSELF

Some company 401(k) and other retirement plans let you borrow money from your accounts on strict terms. Then you pay interest to yourself at the market rate, adding to your retirement savings. The main drawback is that the interest expense isn't deductible on your tax return, even if you use the money to buy or improve your home.

You can't borrow from your IRA. But there's an interest-free way to have temporary use of the money if you're sure you can pay it all back within 60 days. The law lets you withdraw money from an IRA once in a 12-month period without tax or penalty if you "roll it over"—or transfer it—to another IRA within 60 days. If you miss the deadline, you will owe tax and perhaps an early-distribution penalty.

The law permits similar arrangements, known as 403(b) plans, for teachers, church workers and employees of other non-profit organizations.

INDIVIDUAL RETIREMENT ACCOUNTS

An IRA is a retirement-savings plan that you set up and run yourself. It's most

THE LONGER YOU DEFER THE MORE YOU SAVE*

Years	Taxable (after taxes)	Tax-deferred (before taxes)	Tax-deferred (after taxes)
10	$ 13,802	$ 16,470	$ 14,141
20	$ 19,048	$ 27,127	$ 20,961
30	$ 26,289	$ 44,678	$ 32,194

*Based on $10,000 investment earning 5% interest compounded monthly, and taxed at 36%.

WITH A TAX-DEFERRED PLAN...

YOU PAY NO TAX ON ALL EARNINGS UNTIL YOU WITHDRAW

for example

$	10,000	invested
+	34,678	30 years of tax-deferred earnings at 5%
=	44,678	total value
−	12,484	federal taxes collected on earnings when you withdraw at 36%
= $32,194	**WHAT'S LEFT AFTER TAXES**	

TAX SAVINGS $5,905

valuable if you aren't covered by a company plan, but you can have an IRA in addition to a company plan. See IRS Publication 590, "Individual Retirement Arrangements."

The maximum annual contribution to an IRA is the lesser of your annual pay (plus alimony income) or $2,000—a total of $4,000 for working spouses. If you file a joint return with a non-working spouse, you can put a combined total of $2,250 a year into separate IRAs.

At its best, an IRA provides a tax deduction for your contributions and tax deferral for its earnings. You don't pay tax on the contributions and earnings until you withdraw them.

However, if either you or your spouse is covered by a company retirement plan, you may lose the deductions for your contributions. Even so, you still benefit from the tax deferral. If you paid your tax on the contributions up front, you don't have to pay taxes on withdrawals except on their earnings.

IRA deductions for workers and their spouses already covered by company plans are phased out as adjusted gross income, or AGI, rises. There's no IRA deduction for a single person with an AGI of $35,000 or more, or for a married couple filing jointly with an AGI of $50,000 or more.

Remember also that non-deductible IRAs require more paperwork. You have to file Form 8606 with your tax return. Withdrawals are especially complicated if they combine taxable and tax-free amounts. If you can't deduct an IRA, you may be better off contributing all you can to company-sponsored plans.

SIMPLIFIED EMPLOYEE PENSIONS, OR SEPS

SEPs are programs for employers that don't have company plans. An employer contributes tax-deferred dollars to individual retirement accounts for the employees. If there are no more than 25 employees in the company, they may contribute tax-deferred dollars out of their paychecks.

SEPs can accomodate larger contributions than IRAs. You can save money and professional fees with SEPs because filing requirements are simpler than those of other plans.

Self-employed people can use SEPs, too.

KEOGH PLANS

Self-employed people in unincorporated businesses such as sole proprietorships and partnerships can set up Keogh plans for themselves and their employees. Taxes are deferred on contributions to a plan and on its earnings.

You'll need professional help to set up a Keogh plan. The maximum contribution, a percentage of your pay, is tricky to figure. The absolute maximum is $30,000 a year. See IRS Publication 560, "Retirement Plans for the Self-Employed."

You may use a Keogh plan if you are an employee covered by a company retirement plan, but run your own part-time business on the side. Putting self-employment income into a Keogh plan can bolster your retirement savings and reduce your current taxes.

Tax Planning for Investments

Don't overlook the tax consequences when figuring the return on your investments.

Financial advisers recommend that you make investment choices based on factors such as return on investment, level of risk and portfolio diversity— not on tax avoidance. Still, investing your money to gain the best possible return after taxes is a vital part of any investment decision.

CAPITAL GAINS

A **capital gain** is the profit that results from buying and selling stock or property. Capital assets include everything you own for investment and personal use—stocks and tax-exempt bonds, your home and furnishings, jewelry, cars and collectibles.

Gains from selling these assets are usually taxable. Losses are not deductible unless you show you held the item for investment and not for personal use. You also need complete records for all of these transactions and expenses. See IRS Publication 550, "Investment Income and Expenses."

A capital gain is the profit produced by buying and selling stock or property.

LONG- AND SHORT-TERM GAINS

If you hold an asset for a year or less, any increase or **appreciation** in its value will result in a short-term gain. Short-term gains are taxed at your highest ordinary income-tax rate. But an asset you hold for more than a year is a **long-term gain** and is taxed at a maximum rate of 28 percent. If the asset was a gift, you add the prior owner's holding period to yours. If you inherited it, you start a new holding period.

A long-term gain is taxed like ordinary income for taxpayers in the 15 and 28 percent brackets. The 28 percent maximum is a boon for people whose marginal tax rate is 31 percent, 36 percent or 39.6 percent.

DEDUCTING CAPITAL LOSSES

You combine short-term gains and losses to see if you have a net loss. The same goes for long-term gains and losses. If you have an overall net loss, you may deduct it from ordinary income (your salary, for example) up to a maximum of $3,000 in one year ($1,500 if you're married, filing separately). If your loss is greater than what you are allowed to deduct, you carry over the excess and deduct it in later years.

FIGURING GAIN OR LOSS

You figure gain or loss by subtracting your **basis** from the proceeds of a sale. Basis is the price paid for the item, plus the expenses of buying, holding and selling it. For example, the commissions and costs of an investment transaction are subtracted from the proceeds of a sale when you figure a gain or loss. If you received the item as a gift, your basis is the same as the giver's was. Use the fair market value on the date you received it if the gift is worth less than the giver's basis when you compute a loss. If you inherit an asset, your basis is the market value on the date of the giver's death. See IRS Publication 551, "Basis of Assets."

PROCEEDS	The amount you get when you sell your asset
- BASIS	The original cost of the asset, plus the cost of buying, holding and selling it
= GAIN or **LOSS**	

Here's how you would figure a capital gain:

	$ 22,000	Gross proceeds from the sale of stock
-	20,000	Amount you paid for the stock
-	385	Broker's commission and fees on sale
=	$ 1,615	Your Capital Gain

THE LONG AND THE SHORT OF IT

An investor in the 36% tax bracket sells stock resulting in a capital gain of $20,000. She saves $1,600 if she has a long-term gain.

SELL ON OR BEFORE ONE YEAR

$20,000 taxed at 36%

= $7,200 TAX DUE

SELL AFTER ONE YEAR

$20,000 taxed at 28%

= $5,600 TAX DUE

HOLDING STOCKS DEFERS CAPITAL-GAINS TAXES

Short-term gains are taxed at your highest income-tax rate.

Long-term gains are taxed at a maximum rate of 28%

While you're holding an investment, you don't pay any tax on its increase in value. The market price of a stock you bought for $5 a share may climb to $50, but the tax on that capital gain is deferred until you sell the stock and collect the proceeds. If you've held the stock for more than a year, the maximum capital-gains rate is 28 percent.

For this reason, well-off investors often pick stocks for long-term growth prospects rather than for regular dividends. Dividends are taxed as they're paid and at high ordinary-income rates.

TAX SHELTERS AND PASSIVE INCOME

Passive income or **losses** come from businesses in which you aren't an active participant. These include limited partnerships, rental real estate and other rental activities that you don't help manage. See IRS Publication 925, "Passive Activity and At-Risk Rules."

Most tax shelters are passive partnership ventures designed to let investors deduct or take tax credits for more dollars than they actually put up in cash. Shelters are designed for high-income taxpayers willing to take risks.

The 1986 tax act eliminated most of these tax shelters. Losses from passive investments may now be deducted only from income from similar ventures. The losses can no longer shelter other income. That is, they can't be deducted from active income, such as wages and salaries, or portfolio income, such as interest, dividends and capital gains. Losses not taken can only be deducted when the passive investment is sold or disposed of in a taxable transaction. A gift is not a taxable transaction.

TAX-DEFERRED ANNUITIES

Insurance companies sell a variety of **annuity contracts**. You pay premiums that earn income, but the tax on the income is deferred until you withdraw your savings. Variable-annuity contracts let you invest premiums in mutual funds.

Annuity contracts may carry heavy fees. It's usually best to invest as much as possible in company retirement plans and IRAs and then consult a financial adviser about the costs and benefits of an annuity.

THE GAIN OF GIVING

If you donate appreciated property, such as stock or a house, that you've held for over a year, you may deduct the market value and avoid capital-gains tax on the appreciation. If a stock's value has dropped, you can sell it, take the capital loss and donate the proceeds of the sale.

Once your child is over age 14, you can save taxes by giving the child stock that has appreciated in value while you owned it. The child sells the shares and pays capital-gains tax at a lower rate than yours.

The 1993 tax act provides a 50-percent capital-gains tax exemption for investors in certain new small businesses.

GRAND OPENING

Tax-Free Investments

Federal, state and local governments pay interest that is partly or fully tax-free. For some taxpayers, these are some of the best investments around.

"Munis" is a catch-all term for bonds sold by state and local governments. The interest they pay is generally exempt from federal tax and is usually exempt from state and local taxes if the bonds are issued in your home state. If you sell munis for a profit, however, you'll have to pay a capital-gains tax.

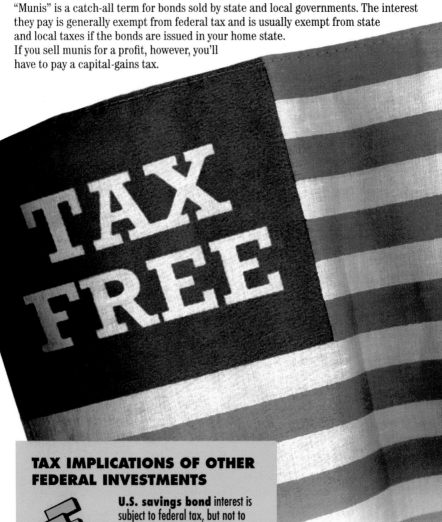

TAX IMPLICATIONS OF OTHER FEDERAL INVESTMENTS

 U.S. savings bond interest is subject to federal tax, but not to state and local taxes. You can elect to pay tax annually or defer it until maturity.

 **Federal zero-coupon bonds** pay you no interest until maturity. But you pay annual federal tax on the interest as though you received it each year.

 Ginnie Mae securities, issued by the Government National Mortgage Association, are shares in the income from a pool of mortgages. The interest is subject to federal, state and local income taxes.

Municipal bonds, like any investment, are not risk-free. Tax-free bonds that pay the highest interest are issued by governments and agencies with low credit ratings. Financial advisers suggest sticking to highly rated bonds unless you're ready to take risks.

Some mutual funds invest only in tax-exempt bonds. Form 1099-DIV will tell you whether your income is tax-exempt or not.

If you're receiving Social Security benefits, tax-exempt income is added back to your other income to determine whether your Social Security income is taxable.

> **Although the interest on state and local bonds is tax-free, you must report it on your return.**

TREASURY OFFERINGS

Investments in U.S. Treasury securities are considered to be the safest available. The interest is subject to federal income tax—but not to state and local taxes.

Treasury bills have terms of up to a year. **Treasury notes** have terms from two to 10 years, and **Treasury bonds** have terms of more than 10 years. Interest on notes and bonds is taxed annually, but interest on bills is taxed at maturity, or when the bills are sold.

FIGURING YOUR YIELD

Before buying tax-free bonds, you need to know whether the **yield**, or interest rate of income, is better than the after-tax yield on a corporate bond or on another taxable investment. Take federal, state and local tax rates into account, especially in high-tax states such as California and New York.

Tax-free bonds may not offer much advantage if you're in the 28 percent federal tax bracket. But the higher your marginal tax rate is, the more likely you are to receive a greater net yield on a tax-free investment than on one that's taxed.

A taxpayer in the 31 percent bracket, for example, needs a taxable return of about 8.69 percent just to match a tax-free yield of 6 percent. But if you're in the 36 percent bracket, you'll need to find a taxable return of 9.37 percent just to equal that 6 percent tax-free yield. These numbers don't reflect state and local taxes or what happens when you receive Social Security benefits. The taxable return must be even higher if you take those factors into account.

Where You Gain on Tax-Free Investments

By finding the number where your tax bracket and tax-free yield intersect, you will see what percentage a taxable investment must pay to equal the tax-exempt yield.

> **An investor in the 36% bracket with a 7% tax-free yield will get the equivalent of a 10.93% taxable yield.**

YOUR TAX BRACKET		15.0%	28.0%	31.0%	36.0%	39.6%
TAX-FREE YIELD*	5%	5.88	6.94	7.25	7.81	8.28
	6%	7.06	8.33	8.69	9.37	9.93
	7%	8.24	9.72	10.14	10.93	11.59
	8%	9.41	11.11	11.59	12.50	13.25

Use the chart above or the formula below to calculate the equivalent taxable yield for your tax-exempt investment.

$$\frac{\text{TAX-FREE YIELD}}{100 - \text{YOUR TAX RATE}} = \text{EQUIVALENT TAXABLE YIELD}$$

Here's how to use the formula. Let's say you're trying to figure how much taxable yield you need to equal a tax-free investment yielding 7 percent. If you're in the 36 percent bracket, here's what the calculation looks like:

$$\frac{7}{100 - 36} = 10.93\% \quad \text{EQUIVALENT TAXABLE YIELD}$$

* Source: *The Ernst & Young Tax-Saving Strategies Guide 1994*, published by John Wiley & Sons, Inc.

Home Advantage

The home you own isn't just a roof over your head. It's a tax shelter, too.

Tax deductions for home loans and real-estate taxes are among the best tax breaks available. You can deduct interest payments on as much as $1 million of the money you borrow to buy, build or improve your main residence and one other home.

HOME-EQUITY LOANS

You can also deduct the interest on home-equity loans of up to $100,000. This kind of loan is like a second mortgage, secured by the value of your home. The amount is based on the market value of the home, less what you owe on your first mortgage.

The big tax break is that you may use the loan money for just about anything and still deduct the interest. You can buy a car, finance a college education, or pay off credit cards. See IRS Publication 530, "Tax Information for First-Time Homeowners," and Publication 936, "Home Mortgage Interest Deduction."

If you use a loan secured by your home to provide money for investments or for your business, the interest may be deductible as investment interest or business interest. The deduction won't be limited by the $100,000 ceiling.

The risk of home-equity loans is putting up your home as security. You can lose your home if you can't keep up with the loan payments.

REFINANCING YOUR MORTGAGE

If you refinance your mortgage, your new deduction is limited to the interest on an amount equal to the principal you've paid off. Let's say you refinance a $100,000 mortgage after 10 years. You've reduced the principal to $90,000, but you borrow $100,000 and pay off the first loan. Generally, you may deduct interest paid on $90,000 as the refinanced mortgage and $10,000 as a home-equity loan. The alternative minimum tax also limits interest deductions if you borrow more than you owed on your old mortgage and you didn't spend the proceeds on home improvement.

Remember that if you refinance to pay a lower interest rate, you also will reduce your interest deductions. That can increase your tax, although the overall effect should be money saved.

If you refinance to cut down on your monthly interest expenses, you are also trimming your interest deductions. That can increase your tax.

SELLING YOUR HOME

The tax law is tough on home sellers. If you make a profit selling your primary home, it is taxable as a capital gain. If you sell at a loss, the loss isn't deductible.

Most home sellers can avoid ever having to pay the tax on the profit, however, by spending all the sale proceeds on buying and improving another home. The proceeds, or **adjusted sales price**, are what you get after you subtract selling costs.

Generally, you can "roll over" the gain on the sale of your home and defer the tax no matter how many times you move,

THE BENEFITS OF HOME-EQUITY LOANS

Let's say an appraiser puts the market value of your home at $600,000. You owe $300,000 on first-mortgage and home-improvement loans. Your equity is $300,000. You can get the maximum home-equity loan of $100,000, send your kids to college, and deduct all the interest.

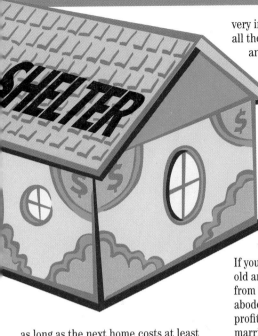

very important to have good records of all the money you spend to buy, sell and improve homes. Those expenses reduce your potential profit.

Unfortunately, maintenance such as painting and repairs such as patching the roof don't count as improvements.

Keep home-sale records as long as you own the home or a replacement. Figuring the profit from selling a home is tricky, especially if you roll it over more than once. See IRS Publication 523, "Selling Your Home."

WHEN YOU'RE 55

If you or your spouse is at least 55 years old and you don't put all of the proceeds from the sale of your home into a new abode, you can stroll away with a tax-free profit of up to $125,000 ($62,500 if you're married and filing a separate return). This could be the best tax break you ever get—and you'll get it only once in your lifetime. If you're married, you and your spouse get the break only once.

as long as the next home costs at least as much as the price you got for the one before. This tax deferral applies to the sale of only your main home—not to other residences such as a vacation cabin.

The restrictions are:

- **You must buy and move into the new home within two years before or two years after selling the previous home.**

- **You can roll over the gain only once every two years unless you move because your job location changes.**

If you die and leave your home to an heir, the deferred taxes owed on past home sales are wiped off the slate and are never paid.

If you don't buy another home after you sell, or if you don't put all your profit into the next one, you owe tax. That's why it's

for example		
FOR SALE	$ 80,000	original purchase price
	+ 20,000	improvements and closing costs
	= $ 100,000	cost of owning and selling your home (your cost basis)
SOLD	$ 250,000	selling price
	– 100,000	cost of owning and selling your home (your cost basis)
	= $ 150,000	PROFIT

If you're 55 or older, $125,000 of your profit is tax free

If you and the person you plan to marry are both over age 55, each of you can sell your home before the wedding and take advantage of a $125,000 tax exemption. However, you must occupy as well as own the property for at least three of the five years before the sale, unless you spend two of the three in a health-care facility.

If your profit is more than $125,000, you can elect to take the full $125,000 exemption and defer tax on the rest of the profit by investing the rest in another home. But if you use only part of the $125,000 exemption—say $50,000—the rest is lost. You'll never get another chance to take it.

POINTS

Points are prepaid interest on a mortgage. You generally can deduct the full amount in the year you paid the points if you use the loan to buy or improve your home. Your lender shows the points you paid on Form 1098, the tax form for mortgage-interest payments.

Deductions of points paid in refinancing a mortgage generally must be spread over the full term of the loan. But if you refinance again, or if you sell your home and pay off the mortgage, then you can deduct all of the remaining points at once.

Marriage and Divorce

Tax planning can soften the blow when divorce settlements favor one party over the other.

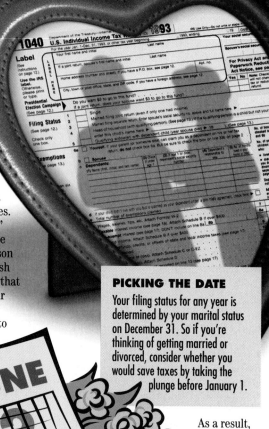

In general, married couples filing jointly pay at a lower tax rate than singles and unmarried heads of household. Several tax benefits—such as the dependent-care credit—are available to couples only if they file a joint return.

There are exceptions to this rule of thumb. A high-income working couple who each earn about the same amount may pay more taxes on a joint return than on separate ones. This so-called "marriage penalty" became especially heavy after the 1993 tax-rate increases. The reason is that combined income may push couples over the new thresholds that raise their tax rate and curb their exemptions and deductions.

If you're married, you'll have to figure your taxes both ways—jointly and separately— to learn which is better for you. You may be able to save taxes by filing separate returns and allotting medical, casualty-loss or miscella-neous deductions to the return showing less income whenever possible. That way, you may come in under the deduction limits that you would exceed on a joint return.

PICKING THE DATE

Your filing status for any year is determined by your marital status on December 31. So if you're thinking of getting married or divorced, consider whether you would save taxes by taking the plunge before January 1.

As a result, both parties need expert guidance to negotiate an agreement that divides tax benefits and liabilities. It's especially important to make clear in any divorce agreement how property is divided. See IRS Publication 504, "Divorced or Separated Individuals."

UNMARRIED PARTNERS

If the state where you live treats common-law marriage the same as legal marriage, federal law lets an unmarried couple file a joint return. Otherwise, unmarried couples who live together file as singles.

Unmarried couples do not have the right to bequeath, or pledge in their will, their estates to each other free of federal estate tax.

DIVORCE

When couples divorce, tax planning can preserve income and assets for both ex-spouses. Without planning, money that could have supported an ex-spouse or the couple's children may be lost to taxes.

LEGAL FEES

In a divorce, legal fees generally aren't deductible. But fees for tax advice and the collection of alimony may be deductible.

ALIMONY

Alimony is tax-deductible for the spouse who pays it and taxable to the one who receives it. For this reason, the recipient who depends on alimony should negotiate for the after-tax amount during the divorce proceedings.

The tax code doesn't condone schemes where one ex-spouse pays the other a big lump of alimony up front to get the deduction. Here's what happens if you do that: Say your divorce settlement calls for you to pay your ex-spouse $150,000 in alimony over three years. If you pay $100,000 in the first year, $50,000 in the second and nothing in the third, the IRS will make you **recapture** a chunk of the $150,000 in the third year and pay tax on it. At the same time, your ex-spouse will get a deduction for the recaptured amount.

You can avoid this trap by giving your former spouse $50,000 a year for three years. The tax law does, however, provide a little leeway. You could pay up to $15,000 of "excess alimony" in each of the first two years without having to recapture—or pay taxes on—the excess. The payments would be tax deductible.

Also, there's no recapture if your payments stop because you or your ex-spouse dies or because your ex-spouse remarries before the end of the third year.

CHILDREN OF DIVORCE
Child-support payments are not alimony. They are not deductible by the payer or taxable to the recipient. The payments must be clearly specified as such, and not as alimony in the divorce agreement. The agreement can specify which parent gets to claim dependency exemptions and child-care credits for the children.

THE INNOCENT SPOUSE
If you and your spouse sign a joint return, you both owe the entire tax. If the tax isn't paid or if the IRS discovers that more is owed, it will contact both of you to collect. It doesn't matter who prepared the return or if one of you knew nothing about it. The law also doesn't care if you later get divorced.

A spouse may escape liability for the tax by proving that he or she signed the return under duress or threats of harm, but that can be hard to prove.

Another way is to prove that you are an "innocent spouse." You must show that your joint tax return understated tax by at least $500 because of gross error or finagling by your spouse. Then you must show that you didn't know or have reason to know of the shortfall, that you didn't benefit from it and that it would be unfair to hold you liable for it. Since this is difficult to prove, you should seek legal advice.

TIMING PROPERTY SALES

If property— perhaps a home— must be sold as part of a divorce, figure whether the tax will be higher if the property is sold before or after the divorce. When a couple over the age of 55 sell their home after a divorce, each person may claim the $125,000 one-time exemption for profit on the sale (see p. 107).

DIVIDING RETIREMENT PLANS

Dividing future payouts from retirement plans is tricky. An ex-spouse may need what's known as a **qualified domestic relations order** from a court to be sure of collecting a share of the other party's pension.

Children

Kids can bring you joy, responsibilities and tax-planning opportunities.

The government looks kindly upon marriage and children. Major tax breaks are available to parents, who can save on taxes by giving money to their children and even by hiring them. A key to family tax planning is the children's age.

TRANSFERRING MONEY TO CHILDREN

You may be able to reduce overall family taxes by shifting some of your taxable income to children aged 14 and older. This works because these children are taxed at their own rate—which is typically lower than the parents' rate.

A child under age 14 with unearned (investment) income over $1,200 is taxed at the parents' rate. So you benefit from shifting income to a child under 14 only if the income is under this limit. Giving a child tax-exempt bonds doesn't shift taxable income. But the child may pay a lower capital-gains tax than you when the bonds are sold.

State laws, called the Uniform Gifts to Minors Act and the Uniform Transfers to Minors Act, let parents and others give money to a child under a custodian's control. Banks and financial-services companies have information about the way these accounts work.

You and your spouse can each give up to $10,000 a year (in addition to normal support) to a child—or anyone else—without federal gift taxes. Remember that legally the money becomes the child's. You can't decide how it's spent after the child reaches legal age.

Trusts are not the effective savings tools for children they once were, because they are now subject to higher tax rates. For 1994, the rates for trusts start at 15 percent, but quickly reach 39.6 percent on income above $7,500. About the only way to save on taxes is to distribute the income to a beneficiary whose tax rate is lower than the trust's.

CHILD LABOR

If you're a sole proprietor, you can shift income by hiring your children. No matter what their age, they will be taxed at their own low rate on income earned from working. They may pay no tax at all if their income is very low. Meanwhile, you can deduct the wages as a business expense.

If you hire your child, be sure the job is legitimate and that you keep regular payroll records. Your child has to do real work and get paid a reasonable wage. Stuffing envelopes or sweeping up for high wages will raise eyebrows at the IRS.

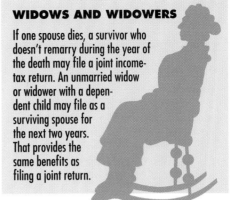

WIDOWS AND WIDOWERS

If one spouse dies, a survivor who doesn't remarry during the year of the death may file a joint income-tax return. An unmarried widow or widower with a dependent child may file as a surviving spouse for the next two years. That provides the same benefits as filing a joint return.

Children who work part-time should file tax returns if they may be eligible for a refund of withheld taxes. They should also consider investing in individual retirement accounts (IRAs). It's never too early to start tax-deferred saving.

PAYING FOR TUITION

Parents can take a dependency exemption for a full-time student under the age of 24 if they provide more than half the student's support. They can continue to take an exemption for a student over 24 whose gross income is less than the personal-exemption amount—which was $2,450 in 1994.

If you have to borrow for your child's tuition, you can use a home-equity loan and deduct the interest. And you don't have to pay tax on scholarships for students seeking degrees as long as the money pays for tuition, fees and books. However, grants for room and board and grants requiring the performance of services such as teaching or research are taxable.

LOANS TO FAMILY MEMBERS

You may want to lend money at little or no interest to a child or a relative. There are generally no tax consequences if the loan is below $10,000, because it comes under the gift-tax rules. But if the loan is larger, or the money is used for investments, the rules get complicated. You may have to pay tax on the "imputed" interest you earn, even though no actual interest is paid.

Any loan you make should be covered by a written agreement, in case the IRS asks questions. If you want to charge less than the market interest rate, you should get professional advice.

RICH KIDS

For 1991, nearly 290,000 children under age 14 reported investment income over $1,200 and had to file IRS Form 8615. Nearly half of those filers reported adjusted gross incomes (AGIs) of under $2,000— but 37 had AGIs of more than $1 million. As a group, the young millionaires paid slightly under $17 million in federal taxes.

Year End Maneuvers

Tax planning at the end of the year can save big tax dollars.

Take income in the year when your rate is low.

for example

A married couple filing jointly has a taxable income of $40,000 this year and expects to earn $155,000 when the wife graduates from business school next year. They have the option of taking a $10,000 sign-on bonus this year, when their rate is 28 percent, or next year, when their rate will be 36 percent. If they take it when their rate is lower, they will reduce their taxes.

Bunch deductions to exceed yearly thresholds.

for example

A couple expect big uninsured medical expenses next year in connection with the birth of a child. They also expect big uninsured dental-work expenses that they can elect to pay for this year or next. If they pay for the dental work this year, they won't cross the medical-deduction threshold. But if they delay the spending until next year, they will bunch enough payments to exceed the threshold amount and reduce their tax bill.

Defer taxes whenever you can.

for example

A self-employed person has the option of taking some income in December or delaying it until January. If he takes the income in December, estimated taxes are due January 15. However, if he waits until January to take the income, he can spread the estimated tax over the next year—giving him 12 months to invest and earn interest on the money. This assumes his tax rate will remain the same.

DON'T TAKE ANY OF THESE STEPS LIGHTLY

Delaying income and accelerating deductions deprive you of money for current investment. Accelerating income to the current year may cause you to lose exemptions and deductions by pushing you over the adjusted-gross-income threshold. More complex considerations come into play if you may be subject to the alternative minimum tax. So it's wise to consult an adviser.

DEC 31

INCOME SHIFTING

Income shifting is the technique of arranging to receive income in the year when you will pay less tax. If you expect to be in the same tax bracket next year, or in a lower one, you may want to defer as much income as you can until New Year's Day or later. That way, you delay paying taxes on the income until the next year, when you may pay less tax on it.

On the other hand, if you expect to be pushed into a higher tax bracket next year by increased income or a tax-law change, you may want to accelerate some of next year's income into this year. Then it will be taxed at this year's lower rate.

If you think your tax rate will go down next year, you can shift income and the tax on it to next year by buying Treasury bills that mature next year. You can do the same thing with some short-term bank certificates of deposit.

Income shifting usually involves a bonus, a capital gain or a payment for services that you can opt to receive either in December or January. There are rules which limit your ability to shift income from year to year. Consult a tax adviser.

BUNCHING DEDUCTIONS

You may be able to shift itemized deductions, too, to trim your taxable income in a higher-tax year. Consider **accelerating deductions** before the end of the year if you see that your tax bracket for this year will be the same as next year's or higher. Or delay deductible spending if you foresee a big jump in income next year.

Shifting deductions isn't easy. But perhaps you can bunch enough medical expenses in one year to cross the threshold for deducting them. You also have control over your charitable gifts.

A check dated and mailed on December 31 or a credit-card charge dated December 31 generally is deductible in that year.

Remember that certain deductions are phased out for upper-income people—those whose adjusted gross income exceeded $111,800 in 1994. You don't want to shift deductions into a year when you will lose them because of high income.

SALE OF SHARES

When the end of the year approaches, add up your capital gains and losses. You may want to sell more stock at a loss to offset any gains for the year. Conversely, you may want to take gains that would be offset by the losses if it otherwise makes sense to sell.

If you want to take a year-end loss but still want to own the stock, you can sell it, wait 31 days, and then buy more of the stock. If you or your spouse buys new shares of the stock sooner, you'll be denied the loss until you sell the new shares because of the **wash-sale rule** regarding trades that cancel each other out. The wash-sale rule doesn't apply if you take a gain.

If you bought a company's shares at various times and prices and you plan to sell, tell your broker which "block" of shares you want to unload. The amount of your gain or loss will depend on what you paid for those particular shares and how long you've held them.

If a regular stock-sale transaction begins in one year and ends in the next, a special rule applies: The sale is taxable in the year of the trade date, not the year of the settlement date. The trade date is when the broker made the trade, not when you delivered the stock and received the proceeds.

The tax code prohibits schemes that attempt to make ordinary income look like capital gains.

JAN 1

Retirement Taxes

Planning ahead can minimize taxes when you start withdrawing money from your retirement plan.

If you have a **defined-contribution** plan, such as a 401(k), you must decide how to take your money out when the time comes. Not only do you want to minimize the tax, but you also want to avoid the penalties for taking your money too soon or, for that matter, for taking too much or too little. See IRS Publication 575, "Pension and Annuity Income."

There are several ways to withdraw money, so you'll need to figure out the

EXIT UP TO AGE 59½

- Pay 10% penalty for early withdrawal.
- 20% withholding if no direct rollover.

PAY TAX

REST STOP

$ **LUMP-SUM LODGING**

% **TAX-DEFERRED FILLUPS**

RETIREMENT INCOME

implications of each method to know which works best. Your employer should provide some helpful information, but you may still want professional assistance.

LUMP-SUM PAYMENTS

Taking all your retirement money in one lump-sum payment can cost a bundle in taxes, especially if you have to pay at the highest rate. But, if you are at least 59½ years old, you may be able to ease that bite with five-year income averaging.

With five-year averaging, you still pay the tax in the year you withdraw your

lump sum. But you figure the tax as though you got the money in five equal annual installments. That may reduce your tax rate. You cannot use averaging for IRA and SEP withdrawals.

If you were born before 1936, you may also consider 10-year averaging. But you have to use 1986 tax rates, which ranged up to 50 percent. Still, part of your distribution under 10-year averaging may be taxed at the capital-gains rate, which in 1986 was a maximum of 20 percent.

LUMP-SUM ROLLOVERS

If you want to roll over your retirement-plan payout into an IRA, or if you leave your job and have to withdraw the money, you must take precautions to avoid a 20 percent withholding tax on the payout.

You can do this by arranging in advance to have your company transfer the money directly to another plan, whether it's an IRA that you set up or a new employer's plan. The check mustn't be made out to you. It must be payable to the new plan on your behalf.

If you decide to roll over your lump sum into another plan, the 20 percent withholding tax can be refunded after you

SOCIAL SECURITY BENEFITS

Depending on how high your total income is when you draw Social Security benefits, you may be taxed on 50 percent or as much as 85 percent of your Social Security income. You may also be penalized if you go on working after you start receiving benefits. In 1994, people under 65 lost $1 of benefits for every $2 earned above $8,040. People age 65 to 69 lost $1 for every $3 earned above $11,160. After age 70, you don't lose any benefits when you work.

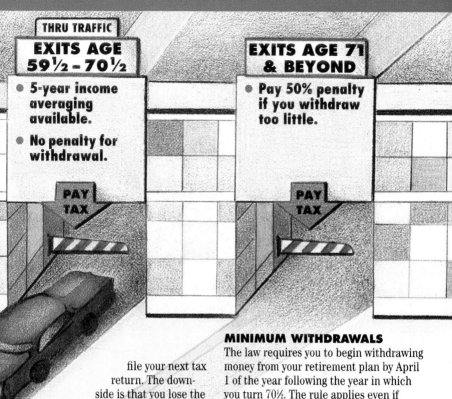

THRU TRAFFIC

EXITS AGE 59½ - 70½
- 5-year income averaging available.
- No penalty for withdrawal.

PAY TAX

EXITS AGE 71 & BEYOND
- Pay 50% penalty if you withdraw too little.

PAY TAX

file your next tax return. The downside is that you lose the use of your money until then. An even more serious pitfall is that the tax withheld is treated as a distribution of income. That means the amount is subject to tax and possibly an early-withdrawal penalty. You can sidestep this problem by depositing an amount equal to your lump-sum payment into an IRA or new company plan within 60 days.

Let's say you receive $100,000 from a company plan and don't arrange for a direct transfer. The company withholds $20,000 and gives you $80,000. But you must still deposit $100,000 in the new plan within 60 days to avoid taxes and penalties. If you don't, and deposit only the $80,000, you'll owe taxes on the $20,000 difference. At 28 percent, the federal tax would be $5,600. If you are under 59½ years old, you may also owe a 10 percent early-withdrawal penalty of $2,000. As a result, the IRS will end up keeping $7,600 of your potential $20,000 refund.

MINIMUM WITHDRAWALS

The law requires you to begin withdrawing money from your retirement plan by April 1 of the year following the year in which you turn 70½. The rule applies even if you are still working. If you don't take the required minimum amount, you owe a penalty of 50 percent of the cash you should have withdrawn.

You may need professional help to figure the minimum amount from IRS actuarial tables. The amount is based on your life expectancy, or on the life expectancies of you and your beneficiary.

EXCESSIVE WITHDRAWALS

If your total withdrawals from all your retirement plans in one year exceed $150,000, you may be subject to a 15 percent penalty on the excess. There are special rules if the amount saved in your retirement plan exceeded $562,500 by August 1, 1986. Even if you use income averaging to lessen the tax on a lump-sum payment, a penalty applies if you withdraw more than $750,000.

If any of these situations affects you, think about withdrawing some money before you retire. Consult an adviser in this case.

EARLY WITHDRAWALS ARE SOMETIMES OKAY

You must generally pay a 10 percent penalty for withdrawing retirement money before 59½ and not rolling it over into another plan. But there are several exceptions:

- You may take the money at any age as an annuity. That means you'll receive equal annual payments based on your life expectancy or on the combined life expectancies of you and a beneficiary.

- You may make withdrawals at any age if you're totally and permanently disabled. Your beneficiary may make withdrawals if you die.

- You may withdraw money from a 401(k) plan if you retire after the age of 55, or at any age if you show a hardship and use the money for deductible medical expenses.

Estate and Gift Taxes

Nothing is certain but death and taxes. The big difference is that some taxes continue even after you die.

REDUCE YOUR ESTATE TO SAVE TAXES

$600,000

THE VALUE OF YOUR ESTATE

Your estate is the total value of all your savings and retirement accounts, your home and any other property, less your debts. If the value of your estate is under $600,000, it will escape federal estate tax when you die. If not, get out your calculator.

CALCULATING YOUR NET WORTH

It pays to compute your net worth. Many people are surprised when they find that their net worth, which is the value of their estate minus mortgages and other debts, has climbed above $600,000.

Be sure to include the amount you have built up in retirement plans, and to get an accurate assessment of the market value of your home and your equity in it. Other assets to consider are your life-insurance proceeds, which could put you over the $600,000 threshold, and any inheritance you anticipate.

If your estate is over $600,000 or seems likely to top that number, you need expert tax advice as well as a competent will drafter. It pays to review your will and estate plan periodically, especially if the value of your assets, the make-up of your family, your wishes or the tax law change.

The worth of your estate property, such as your home or stocks and bonds, is figured at the market value on the date of your death or six months after—not at what you paid for the property. Your executor picks the

valuation date. Current market value may raise the estate tax, but it also means that in most cases, neither your estate nor your heirs will ever pay capital-gains tax on any increased value of the property that occurred before your death.

Under current law, there is no capital-gains tax on your estate.

GIFT TAXES

If you have a large estate, you can avoid estate and gift taxes on annual gifts of up to $10,000 each to as many people as you like. So can your spouse. For example, a couple with three children may give each child $20,000 a year and reduce the potential taxable estate by $60,000.

Gifts above these amounts use up your $600,000 combined gift-estate-tax exemption. The taxable gifts are included in your estate when you die, and generally the gift taxes are credited against the estate tax. However, any gift tax you pay

FROM MOM

ESTATES VALUED OVER $600,000

Estate-tax rates start at 37 percent on taxable amounts over $600,000 and range up to 55 percent on estates over $3 million. There is a 5 percent surcharge on estates over $10 million. There are deductions for certain estate expenses and a credit for state estate or inheritance taxes.

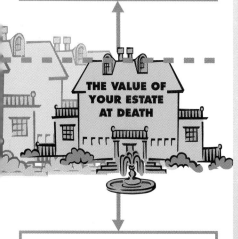

THE VALUE OF YOUR ESTATE AT DEATH

ESTATES VALUED UNDER $600,000

No federal estate tax on estates valued under $600,000.

PLANNING BASICS

- Planners try to arrange estates so that both spouses can take advantage of the $600,000 exemption. The first to die may leave $600,000 directly to children or heirs other than the spouse. Or the $600,000 may be put in a trust, with the income going to the spouse until she or he dies. Then up to $1.2 million goes to the other heirs tax-free.

- Life-insurance proceeds aren't subject to income tax. But they are included in your taxable estate if you own the policy when you die or if you assigned ownership to someone else during the three years before your death.

- If you expect your estate to be taxed, you should arrange for it to raise cash for the purpose. You also want your estate to have cash to pay for your funeral, to pay off your debts and to cover your estate's administration expenses. The estate can deduct these expenses.

- Consider charitable bequests to reduce your taxable estate. Before death, you can use trusts to give property to a charity while taking a charitable deduction and retaining income for yourself.

- Beware of a complicated tax called the **generation-skipping tax** that may apply to gifts or bequests of more than $1 million to grandchildren or great-grandchildren.

during the three years before your death is included in your estate.

In addition to the $10,000 gifts to individuals, you can pay unlimited medical expenses or tuition for anyone—a grandchild, perhaps—without being subject to gift tax. You also can deduct the medical expenses on your own tax return as long as the receiver is a dependent. But you must pay the hospital, doctor or college directly. Don't give the money to the patient or the student.

IRA DONATIONS

Some wealthy individuals arrange to have their IRAs donated to qualified charitable organizations when they die. That way, their estates escape paying estate and income taxes on them.

THE MARITAL DEDUCTION
While you live, you may make unlimited tax-free gifts to your spouse. When you die, you can leave your entire estate to your spouse free of estate tax, provided he or she is a U.S. citizen. Your spouse's estate will be taxed at his or her death.

If a wife and husband own property, such as a home, as **joint tenants with the right of survivorship**, only half the value is included in the estate of the first to die. But the marital deduction doesn't apply to spouses who are not U.S. citizens. The best way to prevent a tax problem is for the foreign spouse to become a U.S. citizen. Lacking citizenship, a foreign spouse may set up what's called a **qualified domestic trust** to soften the tax blow.

If joint tenants aren't married to each other, the whole property usually is included in the estate of the first to die. The estate's representatives can lessen the estate tax by proving that the survivor paid for all or part of the property, or received a share of it by gift or inheritance.

Tax Forms

You can call 1-800-TAX-FORM to order any form from the IRS.

INDIVIDUAL TAX RETURNS

1040 U.S. Individual Income Tax Return

1040A U.S. Individual Income Tax Return

1040ES Estimated Tax for Individuals

1040ES(NR) U.S. Estimated Tax for Nonresident Alien Individuals

1040EZ Income Tax Return for Single and Joint Filers With No Dependents

1040NR U.S. Nonresident Alien Income Tax Return

1040X Amended U.S. Individual Income Tax Return

FORM 1040A SCHEDULES

SCHEDULE 1 Interest and Dividend Income

SCHEDULE 2 Child and Dependent Care Expenses

SCHEDULE 3 Credit for the Elderly or the Disabled

SCHEDULE EIC Earned Income Credit

FORM 1040 SCHEDULES

SCHEDULE A Itemized Deductions

SCHEDULE B Interest and Dividend Income

SCHEDULE C Profit or Loss From Business

SCHEDULE D Capital Gains and Losses

SCHEDULE E Supplemental Income and Loss

SCHEDULE EIC Earned Income Credit

SCHEDULE F Profit or Loss From Farming

SCHEDULE R Credit for the Elderly or the Disabled

SCHEDULE SE Self-Employment Tax

OTHER FORMS

TD F 90-22.1 Report of Foreign Bank and Financial Accounts

W-4 Employee's Withholding Allowance Certificate

W-4P Employee's Certificate for Pension or Annuity Payments

W-4S Request for Federal Income Tax Withholding from Sick Pay

W-5 Earned Income Credit Advance Payment Certificate

W-10 Dependent Care Provider's Identification and Certification

843 Claim for Refund and Request for Abatement

926 Return by a U.S. Transferor of Property to a Foreign Corporation, Foreign Estate or Trust, or Foreign Partnership

940 Employer's Annual Federal Unemployment (FUTA) Tax Return

940EZ Employer's Annual Federal Unemployment (FUTA) Tax Return

942 Employer's Quarterly Tax Return for Household Employees

1045 Application for Tentative Refund

1116 Foreign Tax Credit

1128 Application To Adopt, Change, or Retain a Tax Year

1310 Statement of a Person Claiming Refund Due a Deceased Taxpayer

2106 Employee Business Expenses

2119 Sale of Your Home

2120 Multiple Support Declaration

2210 Underpayment of Estimated Tax by Individuals and Fiduciaries

2210F Underpayment of Estimated Tax by Farmers and Fishermen

2290 Heavy Vehicle Use Tax Return

2350 Application for Extension of Time To File U.S. Individual Income Tax Return

2441 Child and Dependent Care Expenses

2555 Foreign Earned Income

2555-EZ Foreign Earned Income Exclusion

2688 Application for Additional Extension of Time To File U.S. Individual Income Tax Return

2848 Power of Attorney and Declaration of Representative

3115 Application for Change in Accounting Method

3468 Investment Credit

3800 General Business Credit

3903 Moving Expenses

3903F Foreign Moving Expenses

4029 Application for Exemption From Social Security and Medicare Taxes and Waiver of Benefits

4070 Employee's Report of Tips to Employer

4070-A Employee's Daily Record of Tips

4136 Credit for Federal Tax Paid on Fuels

4137 Social Security and Medicare Tax on Unreported Tip Income

4255 Recapture of Investment Credit

4361 Application for Exemption From Self-Employment Tax for use by Ministers, Members of Religious Orders and Christian Science Practitioners

4506 Request for Copy of Tax Form

4562 Depreciation and Amortization

4563 Exclusion of Income for Bona Fide Residents of American Samoa

4684 Casualties and Thefts

4782 Employee Moving Expense Information

4782 Sales of Business Property

4810 Request for Prompt Assessment Under Internal Revenue Code Section 6501(d)

4835 Farm Rental Income and Expenses

4868 Application for Automatic Extension of Time To File U.S. Individual Income Tax Return

4952 Investment Interest Expense Deduction

4970 Tax on Accumulation Distribution of Trusts

4972 Tax on Lump-Sum Distributions

5329 Return for Additional Taxes Attributable to Qualified Retirement Plans (including IRAs), Annuities, and Modified Endowment Contracts

5884 Jobs Credit

6198 At-Risk Limitations

6251 Alternative Minimum Tax—Individuals

6252 Installment Sale Income

6478 Credit for Alcohol Used as Fuel

6765 Credit for Increasing Research Activities (or for Claiming the Orphan Drug Credit)

6781 Gains and Losses from Selection 1256 Contracts and Straddles

8082 Notice of Inconsistent Treatment or Amended Return (Request for Administrative Adjustment (AAR))

8271 Investor Reporting of Tax Shelter Registration Number

8275 Disclosure Statement

8275-R Regulation Disclosure Statement

8283 Noncash Charitable Contributions

8300 Report of Cash Payment Over $10,000 Received in a Trade or Business

8332 Release of Claim to Exemption for Child of Divorced or Separated Parents

8379 Injured Spouse Claim and Allocation

8396 Mortgage Interest Credit

8453 U.S. Individual Income Tax Declaration for Electronic Filing

8582 Passive Activity Loss Limitations

8582CR Passive Activity Credit Limitations

8586 Low-Income Housing Credit

8594 Asset Acquisition Statement

8606 Nondeductible IRAs (Contributions, Distributions, and Basis)

8611 Recapture of Low-Income Housing Credit

8615 Tax for Children Under 14 Who Have Investment Income of More Than $1,200

8645 Soil and Water Conservation Plan Certificate

8801 Credit for Prior Year Minimum Tax—Individual and Fiduciaries

8814 Parents' Election To Report Child's Interest and Dividends

8815 Exclusion of Interest From Series EE U.S. Savings Bonds Issued After 1989

8818 Optional Form To Record Redemption of Series EE U.S. Savings Bonds Issued After 1989

8822 Change of Address

8824 Like-Kind Exchanges

8826 Disabled Access Credit

8828 Recapture of Federal Mortgage Subsidy

8829 Expenses for Business Use of Your Home

8830 Enhanced Oil Recovery Credit

8834 Qualified Electric Vehicle Credit

8841 Deferral of Additional 1993 Taxes

9282 Form 1040 Electronic Payment Voucher

9465 Installment Agreement Request

SPANISH LANGUAGE FORMS

940PR Planilla Para la Declaración Anual del Patrono la Contribución Federal Para el Desempleo (FUTA)

942PR Planilla Para la Declaración Trimestral del Patrono de Empleados Domésticos

1040ES(ESP) Contribución Federal Estimada del Trabajo por Cuenta Propia—Puerto Rico

1040PR Planilla Para la Declaración de la Contribución Federal Sobre el Trabajo por Cuenta Propia—PR

4070A—PR Registro Diario de Propinas del Empleado

4070PR Informe al Patrono de Propinas Recibidas por el Empleado

Tax Publications

Refer to these tax publications for help with specific topics or as general guides. You can also call 1-800-TAX-FORM to order them. They are all free.

GENERAL GUIDES

1
Your Rights as a Taxpayer

225
Farmer's Tax Guide

334
Tax Guide for Small Business

509
Tax Calendars for 1994

553
Highlights of 1993 Tax Changes

595
Tax Guide for Commercial Fishermen

910
Guide to Free Tax Services

SPECIALIZED PUBLICATIONS

3
Tax Information for Military Personnel (including Reservationists Called to Active Duty)

4
Student's Guide to Federal Income Tax

15
Circular E, Employer's Tax Guide

54
Tax Guide for U.S. Citizens and Resident Aliens Abroad

378
Fuel Tax Credits and Refunds

448
Federal Estate and Gift Taxes

463
Travel, Entertainment and Gift Taxes

501
Exemptions, Standard Deduction, and Filing Information

502
Medical and Dental Expenses

503
Child and Dependent Care Expenses

504
Divorced or Separated Individuals

505
Tax Withholding and Estimated Tax

508
Educational Expenses

510
Excise Taxes for 1994

513
Tax Information for Visitors to the United States

514
Foreign Tax Credit for Individuals

516
Tax Information for U.S. Government Civilian Employees Stationed Abroad

517
Social Security and Other Information for Members of the Clergy and Religious Workers

519
U.S. Tax Guide for Aliens

520
Scholarships and Fellowships

521
Moving Expenses

523
Selling Your Home

524
Credit for the Elderly or the Disabled

525
Taxable and Nontaxable Income

526
Charitable and Contributions

527
Residential Rental Property

529
Miscellaneous Deductions

530
Tax Information for First-Time Homeowners

531
Reporting Tip Income

533
Self-Employment Tax

534
Depreciation

535
Business Expenses

536
Net Operating Losses

537
Installment Sales

538
Accounting Periods and Methods

541
Tax Information on Partnerships

542
Tax Information on Corporations

544
Sales and Other Dispositions of Assets

547
Nonbusiness Disasters, Casualties, and Thefts

550
Investment Income and Expenses

551
Basis of Assets

552
Recordkeeping for Individuals

554
Tax Information for Older Americans

555
Federal Tax Information on Community Property

556
Examination of Returns, Appeal Rights, and Claims for Refund

557
Tax Exempt Status for Your Organization

559
Survivors, Executors, and Administrators

APPENDIX

SPANISH LANGUAGE PUBLICATIONS

INDEX

INDEX

INDEX

INDEX

U

V

W

X Y Z

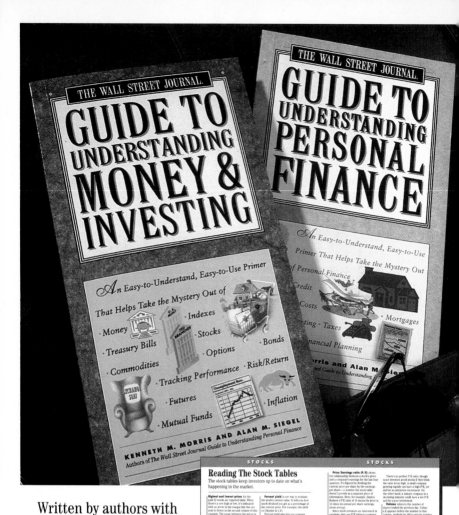

Written by authors with 25 years of experience in the financial and communications fields, these visually appealing, user-friendly guides painlessly initiate you into the mysteries of money and investing. They point out the things you need to know to make smart financial decisions—and to avoid the pitfalls.

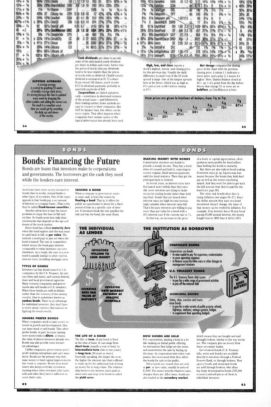

THE ONLY GUIDES YOU'LL EVER NEED TO UNDERSTAND THE COMPLEXITIES OF MONEY, INVESTING AND PERSONAL FINANCE

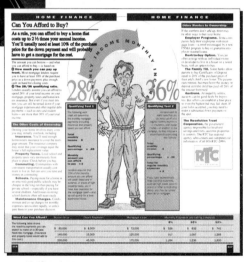

The Wall Street Journal Guides demystify the baffling details and confusing jargon of:

- Banking
- Credit
- Home finance
- Financial planning
- Taxes
- Investing in stocks, bonds, mutual funds, futures and options
- Economic trends
- Financial reports
- Measuring performance
- The global marketplace
- Little known facts about the world of finances

JUST $14.95. AVAILABLE AT BOOKSTORES EVERYWHERE.

Or from:
Lightbulb Press
1185 Avenue of the Americas
New York, NY 10036

Phone	800-581-9884
	212-575-0513
Fax	212-575-2903

Special Offer!

TWO WEEKS FREE!

If you want to learn more about the essentials of tax planning, the Guide you are holding is a good start. But to keep your knowledge up-to-date, we suggest The Wall Street Journal.

Every business day The Wall Street Journal gives you the knowledge you need to make smart decisions about your business, your personal finances, and your career. Three lively sections bring you the top business, economic and political stories of the day, news of how companies compete and consumers react, comprehensive coverage of all the markets. And to keep your tax planning up-to-date, there's a weekly front page Tax Report. See how useful The Wall Street Journal can be in your life. Use this no-risk offer to sample the Journal for two weeks – absolutely free.

Send in this post-paid card today.

YES! Send me two weeks of The Wall Street Journal at no charge. I understand there is no cost or obligation with this special offer.

Name

Title

Company

Address

City   State   Zip Code

Office/daytime telephone

08AP

THE WALL STREET JOURNAL.